Küstenflieger

Küstenflieger

THE OPERATIONAL HISTORY OF THE GERMAN COASTAL AIR SERVICE 1935-1944

ADAM THOMPSON

FONTHILL

FONTHILL MEDIA
www.fonthillmedia.com

A CIP catalogue record for this book is available from the British Library

Typeset in 10.5pt on 12pt Sabon LT Std
Typesetting by Fonthill Media
Printed and bound by CPI Group (UK) Ltd, Croydon, CR0 4YY

ISBN 978-1-78155-283-4

Contents

Acknowledgements

I could not have put this together without the help, support, and general guidance from a variety of people. Irrespective of their input, I want to thank the following for an assortment of reasons. In no particular order, my family Ian and Irene, David and Fiona, David Wadman, Andrew Arthy, Bill Norman, Bjorn Hafsten, Jorn Junker, Hans Nauta, Robert Szoltyk, Larry Hickey, Hans Mcilveen, Marg Castiglione, Robert Forsyth, Verena Pernecker, Remi Trancinelli, Ted Hooton, Ken Merrick, Fernando Almeida, Simon Orchard, a variety of nameless librarians, some keen students, and probably a whole lot more. I just hope I did your inspiration and support justice. But most of all, I would like to acknowledge those who gave their lives for whatever nation, cause, reason, or whim of fate that allowed for this story to be.

I
1918-1933
The Postwar Years

Genesis

The seeds of German naval aviation were planted in a memorandum issued on 26 October 1910 by Admiral Alfred von Tirpitz. Acting as the secretary for the Imperial Naval Office (*Reichsmarineamt*), von Tirpitz ordered the commencement of flight trials for suitable aircraft intended for use by the military. While von Tirpitz' memorandum was not overly specific in either its technical requirements or envisaged roles, it supplied the impetus for further development. A week after the initial order, on 3 November 1910, a second, more specific memorandum was issued, which clearly outlined the German Navy's needs for use of coastal and sea lane reconnaissance aircraft. Buoyed by the success the French had enjoyed in their experiments with shipborne aircraft launched from the old cruiser, *Foudre*[1], Tirpitz was soon pushing the weapons department for similar experiments throughout 1911-12.

In order to facilitate the burgeoning interest in naval aviation, the Germans established a seaplane base at Putzig in the German Bight. It was felt that the region offered optimal year-round conditions conducive for flight, while at the same time was close to North Sea outlets that overlooked main shipping routes. More importantly, the area had primitive facilities from which a permanent base could be expanded. While the region needed developing in order to accommodate any military activity, the location was considered well-suited for its intended task.

Placed in charge of the organisational requirements of establishing a new base at Putzig was *Kapitänleutnant* Max Hering. Although his tenure was only short lived – he was replaced in June 1912 after only a few months by *Korvettenkapitän* Gygas – Hering bore the brunt of the initial

Born 19 March
1849, Alfred von
Tirpitz enlisted in
the Navy in 1865.
In 1897 he was
appointed the State
Secretary of German
Imperial Naval
Office, a post he
retained until 1916.
He died on 6 March
1930.

administrative tasks required in establishing German naval aviation. Yet under both Hering and Gygas, operations at Putzig remained fairly limited throughout 1911-13. For the most part, the training of aircrew was the primary focus. Although Putzig was used mainly as a training centre, some testing of aircraft types was undertaken there. However, despite the potential naval aviation offered, it was not until 3 May 1913 that the decision was taken to expand military seaplane operations.

Irrespective the intentions of von Tirpitz and others, the difficulty faced by the Germans in the lead up to the First World War proved to be mainly bureaucratic. In 1911, the *Reichsmarineamt* set aside funds that ultimately totalled some 200,000 Marks for the development of naval aircraft. In spite of this, production lagged almost exclusively due to the deficiencies of aeronautical and production technology of the time. With such lucrative opportunities, the Navy assumed the aviation industry would be only too willing to be involved. However, it failed to recognise that the majority of German aircraft factories were located significant distances from appreciably sized bodies of water on which to test seaplanes. Moreover, there remained the undeniable fact that land planes were far easier and significantly more profitable to construct than their naval counterparts. Compounding the situation still further, the Navy's insistence that all naval aircraft be amphibious proved such a stumbling block that in January 1913, it had no other option but to drop such a requirement. It was only then that it was able to entice several companies to develop seaplanes designed to compete for naval purchase. It was the two years the German Navy spent pursuing short-sighted objectives that ultimately undermined its ability to field an effective naval aviation force in the opening years of the First World War. In what proved an ominous portent for the future, when Germany marched to war in 1914 it did so with an inadequately equipped naval air arm that had suffered from the short-sightedness of a general staff beholden to economic principles and misguided technological and production assumptions.

By the outbreak of hostilities, German naval aviation personnel strength stood at around 200 officers and men of all ranks. This number did not include observers. While there were around twenty fully trained naval aviators, the naval office had considered training of qualified aerial observers as superfluous. In the event of mobilisation, it had assumed that young officers would be taken from the fleet to serve as aerial observers without any specialist training. Even if sufficient aircrew had been provided in 1914, at that time, all the Germans could muster was the airship L3, supported by six seaplanes on the island of Heligoland for operations in the North Sea. Operations over the Baltic were the domain of the airships PL6 and PL19, themselves supported by four seaplanes at Kiel, two at Putzig, and later eight at Warnemünde. Yet on 19 August 1914, the Imperial Navy had no aircraft serviceable at either Kiel-Holtenau or Warnemünde, while at Putzig, only one aircraft was serviceable. With their limited range and meagre numbers, the Imperial Navy therefore suffered from a lack of useful intelligence in the opening months of the war. This

Early stipulations by the German Navy meant primitive seaplane types suffered from excessive demands that the technology of the time could not meet. One of the early German naval air types was the Albatross WD3, which made its first flight on 5 July 1912.

A map showing the major naval bases of the belligerent forces in 1914. The major British naval base at Scapa Flow meant the Germans needed adequate reconnaissance forces to secure intelligence on the Royal Navy's movements if it was to protect its numerically inferior surface forces.

became painfully obvious with the loss of the cruiser *Hela* and destroyer S-116 by early 1915 to British submarines, which had not been located for want of adequate air cover and reconnaissance intelligence.

With the swift-moving German front soon reaching the North Sea, the German air service, known from 1916 as the *Luftstreitkräfte*, now found favourable opportunity to deploy the majority of its fledgling naval air service units within striking range of Britain. On 24 November 1914, the *Reichsmarineamt* gave the dubious honour for *Oberleutnant zur See* Friedrich von Arnauld de la Perrière – pre-war pilot and brother of the famous U-boat commander, Lothar – to establish the first German naval air unit deployed in times of war on foreign soil. Having established his base at Zeebrugge, by 17 December 1914 von Arnauld was able to report to his superiors that his unit was operational. In an ironic portent of what the future held, demands made by the war on industry, combined with the still relatively slow development in seaplane technology and bureaucratic inertia, meant that the unit was equipped with obsolete aircraft and weapons.

At the same time von Arnauld was building up his command at Zeebruge, construction of an airfield for the Navy in the Oostende area, decided upon as early as 21 August 1914, was under way near Mariakerke. Apart from seaplanes and dirigibles, the German Navy, as with the British, embarked upon the organisation and development of land-based squadrons. In every respect bar the aircraft they operated, these units functioned in the same way as their aquatic brethren. On the same day von Arnauld reported his unit operational, the first unit to occupy the new airfield at Mariakerke – or what was ready of it – began the process of transferring from Snaaskerke, near Gistel, where there was also an aerodrome, to its new home. It was here that the second new naval air unit was deployed under the command of *Oberleutnant zür See* von Skrbensky. On 21 December 1914, Skrbensky arrived at Mariakerke with 113 men and officers and declared his unit operational.

While these two units were far from being the only two naval air units fielded by the Imperial Navy during the First World War, they were the first. Over the next four years, these two units laid the foundation for what eventually would become the *Küstenfliegergruppen*. From torpedo operations against coastal shipping to air superiority operations over the North Sea, search and rescue operations, and anti-submarine patrols, passing through the ranks of these air units were names later thrust into the limelight during the Second World War.

By the end of the First World War, 2,500 seaplanes had been constructed. As of the armistice in November 1918, the *Luftstreitkräfte* had a total strength of 864 front line seaplanes, supported by 16,122 soldiers and

Designed by Ernst Heinkel as a replacement for his Type B.I, the Albatros B.II was a two-seat reconnaissance aircraft. Manufactured before the war, it saw service with a variety of air forces, including Germany and Great Britain.

2,116 flying personnel spread between 32 seaplane stations and 17 land-based stations. While the vast majority of the aircraft operated during the war were seaplanes, as early as 1915 the Dornier firm had built a flying boat, rather innocuously named the RS-I. With an overall length of 29 m and a span of 43.5 m, the RS-I was powered by three motors. While an un-gamely aircraft to look at, and by all accounts to fly, the RS-I provided Dornier with the necessary technical understanding of what was required for the design of successful flying boats.

By 1917, the lessons of the RS-I had been absorbed and used to produce what Dornier termed the RS-III flying boat. On 19 February 1918, the innovative design completed a non-stop flight from Friedrichshafen to Norderney in 7 hours. The lessons that Dornier took from these two aircraft ultimately manifest themselves during the 1930s with the design and construction of the infamous Do 18 and Do 26 long-range flying boats.

During the First World War, the German *Seeflieger* had been responsible for the destruction of some 270 enemy aircraft, six balloons, and two airships. In addition, they had claimed a Russian destroyer, three submarines, four torpedo boats, and 16 other assorted vessels sunk as a direct result of their actions.[2] Crowning their achievement, during the war three *Seeflieger* were awarded the *Pour le Merite*, Germany's highest award for valour: *Kapitänleutnant* das Reserve Friedrich Christiansen (11.12.1917), *Leutnant zür See* Gottahrd Sachsenberg (5.8.1918), and *Leutnant das Reserve*

The usefulness of aerial reconnaissance was invaluable for the war at sea. This German propaganda shot shows a pilot retrieving documents captured by a submarine during the war on Allied shipping.

Theodor Osterkamp (2.9.1918). All these names would again find notoriety in the lead up to and during the Second World War, although in a variety of roles. With the end of hostilities on the morning of 11 November 1918, the German military withdrew from France and the Low Countries, often leaving behind its equipment. Consequently, much of Germany's naval air strength was lost as units began the process of withdrawing into Germany.

Under the Treaty of Versailles, Germany was prohibited from waging war as the twentieth century had come to know it. Articles 198-202 specifically stated vast quantities of aviation material were to be handed over to the Allies, including 17,000 aircraft and engines, with a six-month production ban on civilian aircraft and a permanent ban on military aviation; the effect was catastrophic. With no modern capacity to wage war, the German Army was to be stripped to just 100,000 men, while the Navy was to be reduced to a mere 15,000. The effect was instantaneous. Overnight, Germany was made militarily impotent, unable either to wage war on any scale, defend itself, or even adequately quell the growing rebellion within its own borders.

To enforce such wide-ranging stipulations proved far more difficult than the Allies had originally anticipated. During the winter of 1919-1920, the Allies sent the woefully inadequate force of 383 officers and 737 enlisted men to Germany. To compensate for this relative impotence, the staff of the Inter-Allied Control Commission (IACC), as it was known, were given significant authoritative powers, including, but not limited to, the right

A Friedrichshafen FF.39 floatplane. Developed in 1917, the aircraft was a two-seater used for coastal reconnaissance duties. Aircraft such as these were more often than not abandoned as personnel left their bases in occupied Europe and returned to Germany.

to inspect any military and industrial installation throughout Germany as and when they saw fit. With these powers, it was intended the IACC would control German militarism and any attempts at rearmament.

On 8 May 1920, with the last of its wartime members either transferred to the Army or demobbed, the *Luftstreitkräfte* was officially disbanded. While on paper the Germans no longer fielded an air force, plans were underway within the German military to retain at the very least a doctrinal and tactical appreciation to air warfare as the twentieth century was beginning to understand and explore it. Yet the IACC was doing its utmost to ensure that Germany would soon be without the material necessities for an air force of any kind. By the end of September 1921, the Allied Commission presented a report to the British Air Ministry in London outlining its achievements in disarming Germany of its aerial capabilities. It reported that 574 aircraft (including 58 seaplanes) had been surrendered, and over 14,000 destroyed. Meanwhile, more than 17,000 bombs had been surrendered and more than 214,000 had been destroyed. It had taken the Inter-Allied Control Commission two years since the signing of the Treaty of Versailles, but in that time German aviation had virtually ceased to exist.

Fortunately for the Germans, the Treaty of Versailles provided some opportunity to retain a small portion of aircraft for military purposes. The least of these two opportunities centred on anti-aircraft defence. Although the Germans were allowed to retain an anti-aircraft force for defence, this posed the unresolved issue of how best to train such an arm. While Versailles demanded the eradication of German military aviation, its allowance of an anti-aircraft arm created very real logistical problems within the German military's training establishment. Presenting their case to the Allies, the Germans successfully argued the need for a small force of mostly second-line aircraft for target-towing duties. While these aircraft were all land-based, they did offer the military the opportunity to retain a semblance of air mindedness, if not a very limited training programme. Yet it was the retention of 100 seaplanes along the Baltic Coast that provided the heavily restricted German Navy with the far more advantageous opportunity.

During the First World War, both the Germans and the Allies had sown vast minefields along Germany's coastline. With the war over, these minefields presented a formidable danger to sea traffic that was once again

As the First World War progressed, so too did aeronautical technology. Here, the first Zeppelin-Staaken R.VI flying boat, with the serial number 8301 clearly visible, is prepared for testing operations on the Havel at Potsdam. After the war it was used on a regular basis as a traffic charter, transporting holidaymakers between Potsdam and Berlin to Travemünde.

moving through the area. With the Allies in the process of demobilisation, the task of minefield detection fell to the Germans. While the German Navy carried out the brunt of the work, it proved slow and dangerous. To aid in this work, under Versailles the Germans had been permitted to retain 100 seaplanes purely for the role of mine-spotting. These aircraft were to be based at the seaplane bases near Norderney and Holtenau, and were theoretically supposed to have been either destroyed or handed over to the Allied Control Commission by December 1919. Yet the *Flottenabtielung Referent für Seeflugwesen* (Fleet Advisor for Naval Aviation) and former *Kaiserliche Marine* Staff Officer *Kapitänleutnant* Faber managed, through a bureaucratic slight of hand, to retain no fewer than six of these aircraft in operational condition at various seaplane bases in the Baltic until well into 1934.

Born in Brunswick on 30 August 1888, Walther Faber joined the *Kaiserliche Marine* in 1906. On 1 April 1913, Faber was among the first to join the ranks of the Navy's *Seeflieger* when he commenced his flight training. Having graduated just before the outbreak of war, Faber was assigned to a variety of combat duties. By 1917, he had risen to the rank of *Marineflugchef* (Chief of Marine Aviation), and it was in this capacity that he effectively remained in the immediate postwar period. However, in deference to Allied sensibilities his title was necessarily changed to reflect the supposed absence of naval aircraft within the German Navy. It was due almost entirely to Faber's persistence and dedication to naval aviation that the Navy was able to maintain any form of air mindedness during the 1920s.

While Faber's title was inspiring, any advice he offered on naval aviation proved limited and was often ignored. Unlike the Army, the German Navy did not conduct a comprehensive examination of the lessons of the First World War. Traumatised by the events surrounding the October 1918 mutiny, it had very little to celebrate, the tactical success of the Battle of Jutland notwithstanding. Consequently, despite the valiant service naval aviation had provided during the war, the leading admirals of the postwar Navy tended to overlook maritime aviation, remembering instead the glory of Jutland. For the admirals of the postwar German Navy, maritime aviation was merely a tactical force for fleet reconnaissance, and it was the battleship that was still considered to be the prime offensive weapon for any navy the world over.

These debilitating obstacles served only to make Faber's job of resurrecting the fine traditions of the *Küstenfliegerabteilungen* (coastal flying units) of the First World War ever more difficult. With an Admiralty less than enthusiastic about the development and acquisition of a true strategic naval air force and an overzealous peace settlement, Faber was forced to work alone. With such a low profile within the Navy, Faber found it increasingly difficult to attract significant numbers of air-minded naval officers to his cause. Under the terms of Versailles, the postwar German Navy was allowed to retain an officer corps of just 1,500 men, of which only 20 had any form of aviation experience. This equated to a mere 1.5 per cent of officers, compared with the 5 per cent its Army counterpart retained. By the close of 1921, a mere fifteen pilots were on the Navy's pay role, with only Faber employed in any worthwhile position relevant to naval aviation.

The worsening trend of discrimination and oversight experienced in 1921 partly reflected the worsening aviation crisis within Germany. The only glint of hope was the growing rivalries in the Pacific, which had led to an arms race between Japan and America, both of which sought the design genius of German aeronautical engineers. Despite the climate in which the German aviation industry found itself, it was in light of American and Japanese requests that the famed First World War naval ace Friederich Christiansen convinced Ernst Heinkel to produce an aircraft that Christiansen was sure he could sell to both parties. Working out of an old *Kaiserliche Marine* seaplane hanger at Travemünde, Christiansen and Heinkel, in collaboration with another ex-naval flier Carl Caspar, produced a short-range reconnaissance-type aircraft for use aboard submarines. The U1, as it became known, was a cantilever biplane with a 50-hp engine and a top speed of 140 kph (87 mph). Four men without tools could dismantle the U1 in 22 seconds and stow it inside a purpose-built submersible tank, measuring 5.5 m (18 feet) long and 1.4 m (4.5 feet) wide. Just 33 seconds was required to reassemble the plane ready for takeoff. Realising the potential that such an aircraft offered future naval plans, and in outright defiance of the Versailles ban on both aircraft and U-Boats, the German Navy ordered a single example for testing – its first aircraft designed, produced, and acquired since the imposition of Versailles some years earlier. Due to the success and acclaim of the U1 and a subsequent follow-up design (the S.1 floatplane that Heinkel sold to the Swedes), Christiansen, supported now by Faber (though strictly speaking not as an official naval representative), had no difficulties in persuading Heinkel to strike out on his own as an aircraft manufacturer.

While Faber's involvement in persuading Heinkel to set up his own company offered the aircraft designer the prospects of future military contracts, the German Navy still seemed unwilling to advance the state of naval aviation to any serious degree. While the Versailles ban on aircraft played on naval minds during the period, the willingness to order the U1 signalled, at least partially, the Navy's resistance to the *Diktat*, but more specifically, the acquisition and training of a naval air arm at this time.

While naval files of the period show that the German Navy did not at any stage lose sight of the importance aircraft could play in naval operations, much of it remained lip service to the restricted ideals of tactical fleet reconnaissance. In the meantime, the majority of effort required to maintain, train, and expand naval aviation was left to Faber, assisted only by a few clerical staff.

Despite the restrictions on naval aviation, during 1922 Faber was able to organise the first training course in Stralsund for naval pilots. While the course was of a short duration and only a handful of pilots passed through it, Faber tried to use this first programme as a model for future training operations. Indeed, following close on the heels of the first, in February 1923 Faber organised a second training course for prospective naval aviators. Yet despite the measure of success and recognition German naval aviation was slowly gaining, 1923 saw the economic strangulation of Germany reach its peak. Notwithstanding Faber's progress, the fast-paced events of 1923 once more overshadowed German naval aviation, and at the same time juxtaposed the impetus for its development.

By the close of 1922, inflation had reached such record highs as to be wholly unsustainable. At the end of the that year, the German Government informed the Allied Reparations Commission that it could see no way that it could meet the next instalment of its reparations obligations. While both America and Britain remained passive in their objections, the French immediately ordered the occupation of the rich coal mining region of the Ruhr by five combat divisions, supported by tanks, artillery, and aircraft. This, the French reasoned, would ensure continued German reparation payments. With such an escalation in political tensions and Europe once more seemingly headed toward war, the German armed forces were put on alert. For Faber, this meant an expansion of his operations as the Germans sought to secure themselves against any possible French aggression.

Born in Grunback on 24 January 1888, Ernst Heinkel was a prolific aircraft designer. He was credited with many successful designs, many of which formed the backbone of the *Küstenfliegergruppen*.

Having previously worked alone on naval aviation matters, Faber was now given a staff of four and his operation expanded to become what was regarded as the A1 1I office. While this new office was supposed to handle the expansion of naval aviation in response to French aggression, in theory it provided little more than Faber had previously been accomplishing with a much smaller staff. What the expansion of the naval air office did provide, however, was time for Faber to extend his duties. With more staff available, Faber was now able to better concentrate on policy and management of his office. At the same time, he began to sow the seeds of a revived naval aviation arm. Faber began to publish periodical reports on developments in other naval air forces across the globe, while simultaneously preparing for a future naval air force and its requisite infrastructure. He kept in tact the bases at Kiel-Holtenau and Norderney, while perhaps the most important aspect of Faber's legacy during this period was his cooperation with the Navy's weapons department, headed by *Kovettenkapitän* Waldemar Hirth, to produce a better air-dropped torpedo.

With the French move into the Ruhr on 10 January 1923, the German Navy received funds to purchase ten Heinkel HS 1 seaplanes from the factory's small workshops at Warnemünde. Yet for Faber at least, the new impetus that naval aviation was given thanks to French aggression was short lived. On 1 April 1923, Faber was reassigned as the chief navigation officer aboard the *Medusa* and was replaced at the A1 1I office by *Oberleutnant zur See* Wolfgang Cesar, himself soon replaced by *Oblt.z.S* Werner Goette. Like Faber before them, both of these officers were naval aviators of the First World War, and both were capable administrators, following on from where Faber had left off. At around the same time, the A1 1I office witnessed a bevy of personnel changes, with new operational commands added to the Navy's naval aviation department.

During mid-1923, naval aviation expanded its intended capacity when the two naval commands *Nordsee* and *Ostsee* were instituted under *Kapitänleutnante* Hermann Bruch and Walther Lech respectively. Similar to the Army's *Referenten zb V*, these two new commands – though virtually devoid of aircraft – laid the foundation for future naval air operations by dividing the seas off the German coastline into two distinct areas of responsibility. The *Nordsee* command was responsible for the North Sea and Skagerrak, while *Ostsee* was tasked with part of the Kattegat and Baltic region.

By 1925, with the French threat in the Ruhr having receded, Faber's attempts at forming, if only an unofficial, concept of an air desk within the overall structure of the German Navy began to gain momentum. While Faber had long since been re-assigned and moved from the A1 1I office, the progressive nature of both naval aviation thinking in general,

Despite the production ban on military types, the Germans still gained experience with the Heinkel-developed He 5. Registered as D-1386, this aircraft was one of seven E variants with a BMW VI series engine and carried the civilian registration of D-OXAX. It served in a variety of roles, including with a seaplane pilot training school, and was finally broken up for scrap in May 1936.

and German naval aviation thought specifically, finally added some much needed momentum. In June 1925, the A11I office underwent a significant expansion and at the same time was renamed. This added weight of authority now saw the A11I office grow to *Gruppe* size and become renamed *Gruppe* BSx. This expansion brought with it new responsibility and a change of command. Branched under the *Allgemeines Marineamt's Seetransportabteilung* (German naval office marine department), the new directorate was commanded by *Kapitän zur See* Rudolf Lahs, an ex-torpedo boat officer with no naval aviation experience and the fourth commander of naval air activities in six years. Under Lahs' command, *Gruppe* BSx now included a greater range of portfolios, including military and tactical (*Korvettenkapitän* Hans Geisler), training (*Oberleutnant zur See* Wolfgang von Gronau, later *Kapitänleutnant* Ulrich Keßler), a technical desk (*Korvettenkapitän* Joachim Coeler, later *Korvettenkapitan* Hans Siburg), a section detailing administration reports, and an intelligence desk (*Leutnant zur See* Werener Bartz, later *Korvettenkapitän* Beelitz).

For the next few years, the arrangement worked well, although the state of naval aviation within Germany remained relatively stagnant. Yet with the retirement of Lahs from the Navy in 1929, the naval aviation department again underwent change. At the end of September 1929, Lahs was replaced in command by *Kapitän zur See* Konrad Zander, and *Gruppe* BSx was again renamed, this time to *Gruppe* LS. Partly, these new administrative changes were due to the political requirement of keeping any form of German military aviation from the Allies, but they also reflected the increasingly recognised influence naval aviation was having on the role of naval operations the world over. For the next three years, Zander guided the direction of German naval aviation matters, before on 1 October 1932 he himself was transferred to the post of chief of staff for Inspector of Torpedoes and Mines and was replaced at *Gruppe* LS by *Fregattenkapitän* Rudolf (Ralf) Wenninger.

Despite the best efforts of Lahs, Faber before him, and their staff, when Zander took control he found its operations inadequate to both his liking and the requirements of a modern naval aviation force. Although the naval aviation programme within Germany had only attracted an annual budget of about RM 10 million during the latter 1920s, Zander was able to refine the Gruppe's operation to such an extent that he managed to squeeze a greater effectiveness from it. This more streamlined operation therefore allowed Zander to immediately embark upon a programme of expansion.

Almost overnight, the training time for pilots doubled from six months to one year, while to qualify for the position of observer a recruit had to endure two years of intense training instead of the previously required twelve months. To supplement these extended pilot and observer courses, Zander introduced further training courses for flight engineers and radio operators, which were designed not only to complement aircrew efficiency, but bolster the overall efficacy of maritime aviation as both a separate strategic air arm and a homogenous entity directly linked to the role of the fleet. Overlooking nothing, Zander even found time and resource enough to make provisions within the training system for the expansion of ground crew training. Thus by 1931, German military naval aviation stood on a sound foundation of technical theory and training, supported as far as was possible by a growing base of theoretical doctrine, derived not just from observation of foreign air services, but also the dissemination and dissection of internal theories, papers, discussions, and limited air operations. However, the difficulty still remained the restrictions of Versailles. Although Germany had been allowed to retain an anti-aircraft defence arm and a handful of second line, non-military aircraft for target towing duties, not even the broadest interpretation of these agreements could justify naval air activities of any great extent. In an effort to circumnavigate these difficulties, by 1927 a system had been introduced whereby naval air officers were given ostensibly 'private' training at a naval station at Warnemünde. While this system proved to be sufficient within the context of then-current naval aviation capacity and requirements, by mid-1928 it was in need of an overhaul. At the same time the Navy was making use of its ultra-secret Radio Experimental Command at Warnemünde, the civilian firm Severa (established ostensibly as a civilian air freight company in 1924) was employed as a stopgap measure for the training of pilots and observers. Operating out of Kiel-Holtenau and Norderney, the company initially only offered refresher courses for wartime observers, yet as the demand for naval aircrew gradually increased, so too did the company's naval support operations.

On 1 September 1929, the Reich Defence Ministry informed the German Navy's Fleet Command that, 'The Coastal Air Section, which had been guided by the Navy, was dissolved during the latter part of April for considerations of internal and foreign policy.' While this presented the Navy with a certain challenge, it was instead, 'Able to make a contract with a private air company, the *Luftdienst G.m.b.H*, whereby the Navy will hire airplanes at a fixed hourly rate.' Included in this arrangement were the use of *Luftdienst G.m.b.H* personnel, although only for, 'Those duties only permissible under the terms of the Paris Agreement, including target flights and target towing duties. For all other activities, naval officers are to be assigned to the aircraft as observers.'

While this new arrangement somewhat upset the traditional structure of minimalist naval aviation aircrew training, it did offer some advantages. The new agreement with *Luftdienst G.m.b.H* allowed the *Reichsmarine*'s naval aviators access to 3,000 flying hours annually for 1929, 1930, and 1931. This annual allotment of flight time was to be split up with 950 hours dedicated to the Baltic Seaplane Station, 1,550 hours for the North Sea Command, and the remaining 500 hours for the Naval Command itself. These flight hours were far in excess of anything that the Navy could have ever hoped for without such an arrangement. With such an increase in airtime availability, by mid-1930 the *Reichsmarine* had the luxury of being able to annually select a small number of air cadets from an ever-increasing list of applicants for employment as naval aircrew. This therefore meant only the most qualified, intelligent, and apt students were chosen for inclusion in any air training programme. Built on a solid foundation of personal aptitude, the skills and experience of aircrew chosen for naval service increasingly rose as they benefited from the expanded training curriculum introduced by Zander in late 1929.

By the early 1930s, training for a naval aircrew meant a stint of anywhere up to two years in a training school; a prodigious period by any estimation. Sometimes, aircrew were selected for a brief detachment of up to six months at the Army's secret training and testing establishment in Russia. While the Army's Russian operation offered the chance to expand

Experience with the He 5 allowed Heinkel to develop the He 9. Here one is stowed away in its hangar at an undisclosed location.

naval operational flight experience, it did so only on the concept that the Navy would one day perhaps operate its own fighter arm. As such, while a handful of naval pilots and observers made the journey to Russia, their stay and training there ultimately bore no worthwhile fruit given the direction in which German naval aviation developed.

By the middle of the 1930s, the first stop for a prospective naval aviator was a civilian school, such as Severa or a *Deutsche Verkehrsfliegerschule* (DVS, German Pilot School), which was then followed up by specialist training, focused on the precise requirements of naval aviation and operating in support of either a major naval fleet or submarine force. In order to render such training, the German Navy set up several *Flugzeugführerschulen (See)* (seaplane pilot training schools) along the Baltic Coast at Warnemünde, Pünitz, and Stettin. These operated *Seeübungsstaffel* (maritime familiarisation squadrons) for the development of naval aviators.

From these schools, a graduated marine pilot then went on to a *Fliegerwaffenschulen (See)* (naval aviation weapon school), which was in effect what the British termed an operational training unit. Only after all this training was completed to a satisfactory degree was a naval aviator deemed ready to join a front line unit, although in the early 1930s these were almost non-existent. The front line unit that a new *Seeflieger* was sent to operated in the same fashion as its Air Force counterparts. The only difference was that naval aviation units were under the command of what ultimately became known as the commander for naval air, or *Führer der Seeluftstreitkräfte*.

With an increase in operational aircrew and access to a minimum of 3,000 hours flight time a year, in January 1931 the Navy was able to issue its first regulations concerning cooperation between fleet and naval air units. However, in deference to foreign policy requirements and matters of military secrecy, at this time aircraft were still only referred to as 'motor tenders' in various regulations. For the next two years, the state of affairs for German naval aviation remained in a kind of status quo. With no new developments suggesting the requirement of a heavily expanded naval aviation arm, nor a challenge in political position by the Allies, or more significantly, a challenge in political philosophy by the Weimar Republic, the state of naval aviation in Germany continued with little variance. Thus, by the time Adolf Hitler assumed power in Germany on 30 January 1933, German naval aviation rested upon a firm foundation of commitment and capability. Yet Adolf Hitler's elevation to Führer brought with it a decided change in the fortunes of German naval aviation and a complete redefinition of the role German naval aviation was to play in the ultimate rearmament of Germany.

2

1933-1944
The Nazi Years

Although much had been done in laying the foundation for a naval air service in Germany prior to the Nazi's rise to power, there still remained a severe shortage of aircraft in 1933. For the first fourteen months of the Third Reich, the focus of rearmament was on land-based aircraft. Despite this, on 1 December 1933 the Germans could boast three Staffeln, supported by a test unit. Given the constraints of Versailles, the three combat units were necessarily camouflaged behind civilian titles:

German Naval Aviation Units: December 1933

Unit	Cover name
Seefliegerstaffel Holtenau	Luftdiesnt e. V.
Seefliegerstaffel List	Deutsche Verkehrsfliegerschule GmbH, Zweigstelle List/Sylt
Seefliegerschule Warnemünde	Deutsche Verkehrsfliegerschule GmbH, Zweigstelle Warnemünde (DVS)
Seeflugzeugeprobungsstelle (S.E.S)	Travemünde

However, in 1934 the rate of re-armament quickened and the Air Ministry placed substantial orders for the construction of a variety of types. The programme subsequently became known as the Rhineland Programme, and envisaged by its completion on 30 September 1935 that eighty-one He 60 and twenty-one Do 15 'Wal' would be constructed for reconnaissance purposes; fourteen He 51 W and twelve He 38 fighters would be completed, with a further twenty-one He 59 multipurpose aircraft being constructed. These figures were to prove optimistic, as the constricted aircraft industry struggled to keep pace with demand. Of the 320 He 45s ordered, only 189 were produced in 1934. Predominantly, these aircraft were used by training establishments that supported a growing front line capability, but some were converted to maritime standards.

As the Nazis consolidated their military position and strengthened their air forces, on 1 April 1934 the military structure of Germany was reorganised to accommodate the planned increase in air strength. In an effort to make defence more manageable, six new commands were created to oversee military activity in specific regions (see 'Camouflage and Markings'). While this did little to improve the size of naval aviation forces available, it did allow the Germans to develop a more coordinated approach to military matters. In charge of *Luftkreiskommando* VI was *Konteradmiral* Konrad Zander. While Zander was responsible for all military activity in the region, he was supplied with air operations officer (*Führer der Luftstreitkräfte*) *Fregattenkapitän* Bruch, who coordinated all air activity in the region. It was Bruch's responsibility to mediate between the air service and the commander of the district. Ultimately, this meant that naval aviation was subordinate to the *Kriegsmarine*; a consideration in-keeping with naval theory.

The change in command structure also heralded an expansion in operational planning. The German aircraft industry had struggled throughout 1933-34 in one key area; despite best efforts to rectify it, aircraft engine development and production lagged behind the rest of the industry. This meant that with the introduction of the Rhineland Programme on

From the onset of the Third Reich, the goal was to develop the military. For the Navy this meant the production of the Heinkel He 51W single-seat reconnaissance aircraft.

1 January 1934, the expected production of 149 naval types (along with the conversion of land-based designs, such as the He 45) was well behind schedule. Despite this, by 27 March 1935 sufficient numbers of aircraft were available to allow for the formation of three new units on 1 April. These were *Küstenaufklärungsstaffel* (*Fernaufklärungsstaffel*) 1./126 at List, *Küstenaufklärungsstaffel* (*Mehrzweckestaffel*) 2./116 at Norderney, and *Küstenjagdstaffel* 2./136 at Kiel-Holtenau. The addition of long-range and general purpose reconnaissance units, as well as a single fighter *Staffel*, did not impact greatly the German's operational capabilities. However, authorisation was given to develop three further units in the near future. What did provide the military some breathing space was the development of German civilian firms, such as the Deutsche Luft Hansa company, which began operating mail and passenger services across the Atlantic. In an emergency, the aircraft and crews of the company could be – and eventually were – absorbed by the *Luftwaffe* to bolster combat effectiveness.

In recognition of the failure of the Rhineland Programme to adequately supply forward units, on 1 October 1935 a new production schedule was drawn up. Known as *Lieferplan* Nr. 1, it envisaged the production of 462 naval types, supported by a further 200 training aircraft. This, it was hoped, would allow for a naval air arm consisting of twenty-five *Staffeln* to be completed by the end of 1936. At the same time, the Germans began the process of organising units into *Gruppen*. These units would each have a *Jagdstaffel* (fighter squadron), *Fernaufklärungsstafel* (reconnaissance squadron), and a *Mehrzweckestaffel* (general purpose squadron), and would in turn be overseen by a *Gruppenstab* (group command unit). It was hoped that three such *Gruppen* would then be combined to form a *Geschwader* (*See*) (naval combat wing). In addition to those units already in the German order of battle, by 1 October 1936 it was planned to have established another *Gruppe* while consolidating the current units into a homogenous identity. This would have given the Germans *Stab Geschwader* (*See*) G 116, based at Kiel-Holtenau, and *Geschwader* (*See*) G 216, based at Norderney. The former was to oversee two *Aufklärungsstaffeln*, one at Holtenau, the other at Stralsund, and a *Jagdstaffel* and *Mehrzweckestaffel* at Holtenau, while the latter was in charge of a *Fernaufklärungsstaffel* and *Aufklärungsstaffel* at Norderney, a *Jagdstaffel* at Wilhemshaven, and a *Mehrzweckestaffel* at List. Again, production problems prevented the Germans from reaching their targets. However, other problems loomed large and combined to impede the rearming of naval air units.

With the outbreak of the Spanish Civil War in 1936, the Germans began to focus more heavily on the implementation of land-based strategy. This is not to say, as is often erroneously repeated, that the German High

The predecessor to the Do 18 series, the Dornier J Wal shows the clear lines of the future combat flying boat. This particular example was christened *Tornado* and carried the serial number 299. It crashed in the South Atlantic on 15 January 1936 while serving on mail flights to South America for Deutsche Luft Hansa.

D-AFAR was operated by the Deutsche Luft Hansa and after the commencement of hostilities it was taken over for second line duties. It was destroyed by the Danish resistance in 1943.

Command developed a purely tactical view of airpower; rather, events in Spain and German aspirations in Russia lured theorists and planners away from strategic maritime aviation possibilities. Certainly, this was not helped by the head of the *Kriegsmarine, Großadmiral* Raeder, who anchored his doctrinal thinking to that of fleet strategy. For Raeder, the concept of airpower was useful only for fleet reconnaissance. Ominously, the lack of interest in interdicting shipping by air units was reflected in the design of aircraft currently in production and on the drawing board, and the quantity with which they were being ordered. Support for naval aviation was also not helped by the inter-service rivalry that existed between the *Kriegsmarine* and *Luftwaffe* over control of air units. While the *Kriegsmarine* never questioned the need for an independent air force, it did maintain its right to a purely naval aviation arm subordinate to naval command. As far as the head of the *Luftwaffe* and Five Year Plan Hermann Göring was concerned, 'If it flew, it belonged to him.' The antagonism with which the issue was debated was felt long into the war and contributed directly to the impotence and eventual decline of the *Küstenfliegergruppen* during the Second World War.

Unable to coordinate with the *Luftwaffe* over matters of production and control of naval air units, at the behest of Göring the *Kriegsmarine* transferred between sixty and eighty officers to the *Luftwaffe* in 1935 to fill administrative and technical positions associated with naval aviation. Thus, a naval air staff was slowly developed during the year, which over

The installation of defensive armament in a Dornier Wal.

the next three years worked on plans to expand the force from an initial projection of twenty-five *Staffeln* to a service that, by 1938, was planned to include fifty-four *Staffeln* supplemented by twelve carrier-borne *Staffeln* (slated for service aboard the never-completed carrier Graf Zeppelin). Yet the difficulty this fledgling naval air staff faced was continual interference from *Luftwaffe* planners and the low priority associated with naval aviation procurement.

Authorised on 11 January 1935, the transfer of specialist naval officers to the *Luftwaffe* for duty as observers in aircrew meant that 80 per cent of officers in naval air units with the title of *Beobachter* (observer) would be drawn exclusively from the *Kriegsmarine*. These men would be on a three-year secondment with the option of a permanent transfer to the *Luftwaffe* at the end of that time. Importantly, these men had to have at least three years service at sea as a *Leutnant zur See* and hold the qualification as officer of the watch in a minor unit. In later years, as the *Küstenfliegergruppen* were slowly dissolved, many of the naval observers returned to the *Kriegsmarine,* where they were transferred to the U-boat arm; some even went on to command U-boats in the latter half of the war.

Operations in Spain throughout 1936-39 somewhat hid the growing tension between Göring and Raeder over the question of maritime aviation. Raeder's attempt to resolve the question during a conference with the Minister of War General von Blomberg early in 1937 came to little, and was quickly followed by a meeting between the two heads of service on 11 March 1937. Essentially, Raeder sought to clarify the principal roles of each service, and in doing so define once and for all the role of the *Kriegsmarine* and its need for an independent air service to support it. Certainly, it was Raeder's belief that as the naval theatre of war was a single entity, operations conducted there must necessarily be conducted by a unified command with its own forces and strategic reserve. In essence, Raeder was claiming the *Kriegsmarine*'s right to an independent air service under its own jurisdiction. While Göring remained non-committal, on 31 March the *Oberbefehlshaber der Wehrmacht* issued instructions that noted, 'In the whole theatre of war, the primary task is combat, (a) of the *Heer* against the enemy ground forces, (b) of the *Kriegsmarine* against the enemy at sea, (c) of the *Luftwaffe* against the enemy air force.' The only exception that was noted was the coordination of army and naval forces in defence against enemy air forces attacking troops, ships, or fortifications. Far from settling the dispute, the ambiguity of the memorandum further muddied the waters.

Throughout 1937 and 1938, numerous conferences were held in an effort to finally resolve the issue, with the matter coming to a head in early 1939. On 27 January, a conference was held between Göring and

Raeder in which each side offered concessions, although it was the latter who lost the most. In recognition of the *Kriegsmarine*'s argument of a naval theatre of war as a single entity, Göring relinquished responsibility for reconnaissance of coastal areas in support of naval operations. This proved a pyrrhic victory for Raeder, as he effectively signed away the *Kriegsmarine*'s ambitions for an independent air arm by passing control of all naval air units to the *Luftwaffe*. Although these units were ultimately to be directed by the *Kriegsmarine*, the stipulation that all orders were channelled through a *Luftwaffe* air staff assigned to it signalled the beginning of the end for the *Kriegsmarine*'s fledgling forces.

By the time of what became known as the 1939 Protocol, the pace of operations in Spain were winding down. Significantly, neither the *Kriegsmarine* nor the *Luftwaffe* fully acknowledged the role and importance of naval aviation in the conflict. The naval air contingent, AS/88, had ostensibly been assigned to the theatre to develop experience in maritime operations. This included the testing of weapons and the development of tactics. Throughout the conflict, the Republicans lost 552 ships to all causes – 52 of them to the German naval air unit. However, equipped with obsolete designs, the unit struggled to influence German strategic thinking. The limited success using air-dropped torpedoes and the employment against land-based targets blinded German officials

A He 59 used by the *Fliegerwaffenschule (See)* at Bug. Built on a solid foundation developed in the 1920s, the quality of aircrew passing out from such institutions gave the *Küstenflieger* a firm footing at the beginning of the war. Unfortunately for the Germans, often it was the aircraft and a lack of them that precluded success.

Upon completion of training, pilots celebrated their success with a formal passing out ceremony. This ceremony took place at the *Flugzeugführer Schule (See)* Warnemünde in 1938.

to the importance of a fully-developed naval air force, equipped with modern aircraft employing practical weapons. It was not until 1942 that the Germans acquired a reliable air-dropped torpedo, while throughout its existence, aside from the long-range Bv 138, the *Küstenfliegergruppen* were never in possession of truly modern combat aircraft worthy of the maritime reconnaissance role. Belatedly, Raeder did recognise this; on 31 October 1939, the head of the *Kriegsmarine* wrote to Göring bemoaning the poor performance of naval aircraft. However, with the advent of the Second World War and the associated pressures on industry it caused, by then there was little that could be done to rectify the situation.

While events were unfolding in Spain, and the respective heads of the *Luftwaffe* and *Kriegsmarine* battled for control of naval aviation, the service was expanding. In an effort to consolidate their forces, a reorganisation of air units was undertaken in the latter half of 1936. It was during this period that the first *Küstenfliegergruppen* were inaugurated. In recognition of the coastal reconnaissance role they were to undertake, in

Early production He 42Ds at Warnemünde in July 1935. While aircraft such as these
bolstered the number of types available to the Germans, their limited range precluded
them from anything but perfunctory roles in combat.

July 1936 four new *Staffeln* were added to the German order of battle by
renaming existing units. The first complete *Gruppe* organised in this way
to carry the title *Küstenfliegergruppe* was based at List and carried the unit
designation of 106. Formed in October 1936 by renaming the previously
nominated *Gruppe (See)* 116 units based there, this was not the first
Küstenflieger unit; the first true *Küstenfliegerstaffeln* were the three *Staffeln*
of *Küstenfliegergruppe* 206 and the 1 *Staffel* of *Küstenfliegergruppe* 306.
Again, these units were created by renaming the existing *Staffeln* based at
Holtenau and Norderney, but had been christened in July of that year. Over
the next twelve months, a series of new *Küstenfliegerstaffeln* were added
as delivery of new aircraft enabled an expansion of maritime aviation.
By the beginning of February 1938, the Germans boasted the following
Küstenflieger units located at various bases under the jurisdiction of
Luftkreiskommando VI: *Küstenfliegergruppe* 106 (*Oberstleutnant* Roth),
1./*Küstenfliegerstaffel* 306 (*Hauptmann* Hekmann), *Küstenfliegergruppe*
406 (*Major* Geisse), *Küstenfliegergruppe* 506 (*Major* Schily), and

Küstenfliegergruppe 706 (*Major* Metzner). In addition were the two shipborne *Staffel* of 1./*Bordfliegergruppe* 196 (*Major* Lessing) and 5./ *Bordfliegergruppe* 196 (*Hauptmann* Bertram), *Seejagdgruppe* I./136 (*Major* Schumacher), and the demonstration unit *Lehrstaffel See* (*Major* Hagen). Supporting these units was the logistical unit *Luftzeuggruppe 6* (*Oberst* Moll) and the training establishments *Fliegerwaffenschulen* (*See*) and *Flieger-Ersatzabteilung 6* (*Oberst* Ritter). This combination of units meant that by August, the Germans had on strength a total of 185 naval aircraft, of which 151 were recorded as serviceable at the beginning of the month.

By the outbreak of the Second World War, the number of operational *Küstenfliegerstaffeln* had grown to a total of fourteen. Spread across these units and supported by training and support organisations, the Germans could deploy 240 seaplanes, of which 214 were serviceable. Far from unifying the focus of Raeder and Göring, the advent of war stimulated the latter to renew his grab for maritime air units. On 30 October 1939, Admiral Saalwaechter was forced to admit that those maritime air forces available to him were insufficient to meet the demand of his *Marine Gruppe West*. The sole long-distance type then available, the Do 18, was, Saalwaechter realised, totally inadequate. In the first two months of the war, the fifty-six flying boats available had covered half a million miles, which represented a mere 150 miles per day per aircraft. Ten had been lost and only six had been supplied as replacements. The inability to operate effectively was confirmed the following day when Saalwaechter and his staff were informed that henceforth, those maritime air units available to him were to be confined to reconnaissance; all offensive action planned would be undertaken by air units in the *Luftwaffe*'s own X *Fliegerkorps*. This situation did little to help Raeder's cause. On 21 October, a joint operation by 1./406 and I./KG 30 targeting a British convoy located off Cromer highlighted the deficiencies of inter-service cooperation when it ended in disaster. The plan had called for ten He 115s to attack the shipping first to avoid unnecessary losses due to their lumbering nature. This was to be followed up by three fast-moving Ju 88 dive bombers. Poor timing meant the Ju 88s arrived and attacked the shipping first in the face of moderate defensive fire. By the time the seaplanes arrived, the British had been fully warned and the naval aircrew flew into intense defensive fire. In the ensuing action, four Heinkels were shot down and a fifth was heavily damaged. It was clear Göring's policy of *Luftwaffe* control of naval air units was impractical. The confusion between *Kriegsmarine* and *Luftwaffe* units was a common feature of the early war and was to be played out with much larger consequences in February 1940 when communication failures between the *Kriegsmarine* and X *Fliegerkorps* led the latter to attack two German destroyers, the *Leberecht Maas* and *Max Schultz*. The attack resulted in the sinking of both destroyers and cost the lives of 578 sailors.

By the end of October 1939 it was obvious the current deployment of maritime units was creating confusion, with many *Staffeln* subordinate to distant *Stabsstaffeln*. In some cases, *Gruppen Staffeln* were spread between the two distinct operational commands *Führer der Luftstrietkräfte Ost* and *Führer der Luftstrietkräfte West*. These two commands had been set up on the eve of the war to facilitate better strategic control of units engaged over the Baltic and North Sea respectively. However, it was becoming increasingly noticeable that the two entities were cumbersome and responsible for a variety of communication breakdowns and slow response times from *Staffeln* as their respective *Gruppenstab* tried to coordinate far-flung units. As a result, on midnight of 25 October a complete reorganisation of units was undertaken. While this involved the renumbering of most *Küstenfliegerstaffeln*, it did spawn two new numbered Gruppen, *Küstenfliegergruppen* 806 and 906. While the reorganisation did not effect *Küstenfliegergruppe* 106 or 2./406, henceforth *Küstenfliegergruppen* 306 became 406, the former 406 entity evolved into 506, the original 506 became 806, while 706 and 2./606 gave way to 906. As part of the reorganisation, *Stab./Küstenfliegergruppe* 706 was not reformed – an oversight rectified in July 1940. The reorganisation did little to alleviate the stream of losses suffered by maritime units due to technical problems and enemy action. Hampering operations further was

The long-range Dornier 18 was virtually obsolete by the time war broke out. While its long range afforded good reconnaissance opportunities, its limited bomb load and susceptibility to damage precluded it from effectively influencing the war at sea in the early years. Produced in too few numbers, the type represented the failure of the pre-war years to develop an effective anti-shipping workhorse.

the ferocity of the winter, which closed down many seaplane bases from December until well into the new year.

At the same time, the Germans implemented an aerial mining campaign targeting the Royal Navy. Heavily outnumbered, the *Kriegsmarine* could not possibly hope to compete with the British on the open seas. The Germans believed that a sustained campaign from the air would redress this balance. However, what Göring overlooked was the Germans were not in possession of an aircraft capable of attacking heavily defended warships, either underway or at anchor. The only aircraft available for torpedo operations, the He 115, was only available in limited numbers. Thus, the alternative was to resort to bombing and an aerial mining campaign.

Both the *Kriegsmarine* and *Luftwaffe* believed the recently developed magnetic mine would prove decisive. The LMA (250 kg) and LMB (945 kg) were anchored to the seabed and detonated by the magnetic field of passing ships. This gave them an advantage over contact-type mines in so much as they were much more difficult to detect. So important was its design that permission to use the type was not given until November 1939. However, limited production meant the campaign got off to a slow start. At the end of November, only *Küstenfliegergruppe* 106, 3./506, and 3./906 were available for operations of this nature.

On the night of 20/21 November, three aircraft from 3./906 flew the first sortie, but it became immediately obvious that an aerial mining campaign involved considerable risk. To properly sow the mines, crews had to fly at a height of between 400 and 800 m at slow speed. In total darkness, particularly with calm seas, accurately judging height was difficult. Further complicating matters, the mines were sown using the aid of a parachute attached by a solid piece of salt. Upon contact with the water, the salt would dissolve and the parachute would float away. However, for the mines to function properly they had to be set at a depth of between 5 and 8 m. This placed great importance on navigation, with crews required to find specific tidal areas of the correct depth in order to deploy their cargo. Between 20 November and 7 December, the *Küstenfliegergruppen* undertook six such mining operations, sowing sixty-eight mines; the effort was largely futile. Although the motor vessel *Sussex* was sunk on 23 November by a magnetic mine, the British quickly annulled any advantage the mines offered the Germans when they captured an intact version in November. Despite the German's continued mining operations, the optimistic outlook of it being a serious threat to the Royal Navy was never realised.

The deterioration in offensive capability during the first winter of the war was further hampered in April 1940 when Göring issued a revised armament plan, which placed less focus on maritime aviation than previous

During the winter of 1939-40, the Germans employed aerial mining techniques as a way of consolidating their war on trade. Here an aerial mine is loaded aboard a Heinkel He 115 in preparation for an operation.

programmes. Whereas the final and largest plan had called for a total of forty-one *Staffeln* (not including *Bordfliegerstaffeln*), the new plan allowed for just twenty-seven. The thinning of naval aviation capacity was further hampered in April 1940 with the German attack in Scandinavia. Hard pressed to operate effectively prior to the operation, the inclusion of the Scandinavian theatre taxed the *Küstenfliegergruppen* to the limit. Although they had some notable reconnaissance successes during the campaign, the glaring deficiency in offensive capability was tragically highlighted during the first week of the invasion when German naval forces in Narvik were cut off and all but destroyed for want of true air support.

Although the acquisition of Scandinavian bases allowed an expansion in reconnaissance opportunities, the difficulty for the *Küstenfliegergruppen* remained supply and technology. By 1940, the He 59, He 60, and Do 18 were all obsolete. The He 115 was still a capable aircraft and acquitted itself well, although it was too few in number to be of serious impact. Meanwhile, the newly-designed Blohm und Voss Bv 138 flying boat was suffering a variety of teething troubles as it slowly made its way into front line operations. Then in late June, Göring struck a hammer-blow. With the operations in Norway successfully concluded, the *Luftwaffe* shifted its full focus to Britain. Göring recognised that the losses inflicted in the Scandinavian and French campaigns would seriously undermine any

Other types used in the development of the *Küstenfliegergruppen* included the short-range Heinkel He 60, yet these proved limited in their offensive capabilities and were mostly restricted to reconnaissance operations or convoy escort duties.

The more modern Bv 138 provided the Germans with a very long range reconnaissance aircraft. Powered by diesel engines, it was able to operate at extreme range and refuel from similarly powered U-boats at sea. Initially the type suffered teething troubles but it remained in use throughout the war.

hope he had of a sustained effort against Britain. As a result, he requested Raeder relinquish command of *Küstenfliegergruppe* 806 and the two *Staffeln* 3./106 and 3./906 in an effort to shore up his offensive capabilities. Raeder recognised he had little option and attempted to broker a deal. Flatly refusing the transfer of 3./106 and 3./906 on the grounds they were essential to reconnaissance operations in support of a renewed U-boat offensive, Raeder granted the transfer of *Küstenfliegergruppe* 806 on the grounds that it was to be a temporary arrangement only and all other units assigned to the *Luftwaffe* (notably *Küstenfliegergruppe* 506, which had been transferred to the command of X *Fliegerkorps* during the Norwegian campaign) be returned. Raeder's naivety thus further weakened his air command's ability to operate effectively, as no sooner was permission granted to temporarily reassign *Küstenfliegergruppe* 806 than the *Luftwaffe*, no doubt at Göring's behest, redesignated the unit *Kampfgruppe* 806, thereby terminating its naval association.

The loss of *Küstenfliegergruppe* 806 further compounded a weakened force that was struggling to maintain its operational integrity after the November 1939 transfer of the planned *Küstenfliegergruppe* 606 to the *Luftwaffe* and losses sustained thus far.[3] By the first week of August, only 213 naval air types were available, of which just 170 were serviceable for all operational, supply, and training needs. This figure plummeted to 196 (155 serviceable) on 17 August, leaving the *Kriegsmarine* desperately short of operational capabilities.

Designed as a coastal reconnaissance aircraft, the Arado 95 was used throughout the war, mostly in the Baltic from bases in Latvia and Estonia, and was not withdrawn from service until 1944.

The growing intensity of operations over Britain during the summer of 1940 created further difficulties for Raeder. Göring's determination to raze Britain to the ground meant he needed ever-larger numbers of aircraft and crews dropping ever-more destructive bombs. Throughout September, Göring diverted the supply of aerial mines for use as bombs in his Blitz campaign on British cities. To bolster his weakened forces, Göring enlisted the support of the Führer. On 3 September, Hitler issued an order to Raeder that informed him of imminent transfers of naval air units to *Luftwaffe* command. Ostensibly, the Führer validated his decision by explaining the need to support *Luftwaffe* operations in the lead up to the planned invasion of England, Operation Sealion. Hitler assured Raeder that *Küstenfliegergruppe* 506 (still under the command of X *Fliegerkorps*) would be returned to naval control on 18 September, and once the invasion got underway, all naval air units assigned to the *Luftwaffe* would be returned to Raeder for tactical support requirements of the invasion fleet.

The development of the *Luftwaffe*'s own naval air units further hampered Raeder's claim to authority in the naval theatre. By early 1941, it was becoming increasingly clear that the *Kriegsmarine*'s position was untenable. Göring had successfully manipulated Hitler into issuing a series of decrees, which culminated in a Führer Directive on 28 February 1941. This stated that no plans for a naval air arm existed and that, as the *Luftwaffe* was also engaged in action in naval areas, the weight of authority lay with the *Luftwaffe* and not the *Kriegsmarine*. Thus, those *Küstenfliegergruppen* still under the command of the *Kriegsmarine* were liable for transfer to the *Luftwaffe*. This directive presaged a watershed in the *Kriegsmarine*'s air capabilities. By the end of September 1941, the *Kriegsmarine* had been picked bare, left only with *Küstenfliegergruppe* 506, 1./706, and 5./*Bordfliegergruppe* 196. On 19 October of that year, Göring gained control of *Küstenfliegergruppe* 506. Although the *Kriegsmarine* was able to retain control of its shipborne unit 5./196 until the end of the war, on 13 July 1943 it lost control of *Küstenfliegerstaffel* 1./706 when it was redesignated as the *Luftwaffe*'s own maritime air unit 1./Seeaufklärungsgruppe 130. From then until October 1944, when it was disbanded, the last *Küstenfliegerstaffel* still in combat was 1./406. The loss of 1./406 meant the term *Küstenflieger* had all but disappeared from the German order of battle. Thus, the downfall of the *Küstenfliegergruppen* was complete.

3

Camouflage and Markings

Unlike various other units of the *Luftwaffe*, the camouflage and marking schemes of the *Küstenfliegergruppen* remained relatively stable throughout the period of their existence. Within Germany, the earliest forms of aircraft registration had been devised after the First World War. This form of registration comprised of the letter 'D' for Deutschland – signifying the country of origin – followed by a number based on the order of registration and the class of the particular aircraft in question. This form of registration was applied to all types of aircraft built and registered within Germany throughout the 1920s and early 1930s. With the harsh impositions of Versailles, and later the Paris Agreement, relatively few aircraft were produced within Germany. This therefore presented no particular problem for such a style of aircraft registration. As the Reich Law Gazette No. 78 of 29 August 1939 noted:

> Aircraft carry the national marking D and the registration marking on both sides of the fuselage between wing and tail unit, monoplanes additionally on both surfaces of the wings, and biplanes on the undersides of the lower wings and on the top surface of the upper wings.

With Germany officially denied a military air force of any kind during the period, organised and controlled camouflage schemes for German military aircraft were unheard of. According to the governing Allied Control Commission, the only things flying in Germany during the period were civilian in nature, thus camouflaged aircraft of any kind would immediately have drawn suspicion. Instead, aircraft of the period produced and registered in Germany merely retained the paint scheme that the aircraft had applied as it left the factory. Usually the finish

The port-side of the pre-production Heinkel He 60, *WNr* 438, at Warnemünde. (*Via D.Wadman*)

was a light grey colour, though there were variations on this. While the German Navy did posses several military aircraft, their colour schemes and markings were either left over from the aircraft's previous First World War service, or was an application of a suitably darkened colour embedded in the dope used to fix the aircraft's fabric. While this may not be considered 'camouflage', this early pale grey was a very effective sky camouflage.

In 1925, the *Reichsausschuss für Lieferbedingungen* (RAL), or Reich Committee for Conditions of Supply, was formed, and by 1927 had organised a system of restricted colour use for aircraft manufactures. Initially, the RAL laid down a list of 40 colour shades consisting of 13 primary colours and a further 27 obtained by mixing the base colours. While this colour list grew during the 1930s to include over 100 by the outbreak of the Second World War, the original 40 colours remained the staple colour of the seaplane and flying boat operators during the 1920s and early 1930s.

However, with the rise to power of Adolf Hitler and his Nazi party in January 1933, Germany witnessed a massive revival of its aviation industry and output potential. With Hitler there came a reinvigoration, albeit slowly, in the potency of German naval aviation and its camouflage concepts. Due entirely to Versailles, in early 1933 there were no more than 100 military aircraft available throughout Germany. Essentially, these aircraft, with a few exceptions, were converted civilian aircraft that retained civilian colour schemes.

Employing just 3,988 workers on 31 January 1933, nine months later, on 31 October, the German aviation industry had swelled to a workforce of 11,635. This explosion in capacity brought with it an obvious increase in aircraft production. While the great majority of production throughout the Third Reich era was focused on land-based aircraft, those naval aircraft that were produced during this period underwent several changes

A Bv 138 on the production line in 1940. The workforce and industrial space needed to build such large aircraft in quantity was unavailable in the mid-1930s and hampered the development and expansion of the *Küstenfliegergruppen*.

to their camouflage and markings as military requirements became more pressing.

Hitler's rearmament programme of the mid-1930s gave the German Navy the chance to embark upon a period of expansion, not least of all for its naval aviation units. The aircraft that were now being delivered to the Navy from manufacturers all came wearing a generic all-over RLM 02 *Grau* (grey) finish. The only deviation for naval aircraft was the surfaces that were in contact with water. For seaplanes, this meant the pontoons received a protective layer of RLM 01 *Silber* (silver) and a clear lacquer to guard against the corrosive effects of salt water. This standard paint scheme was adopted by the Navy without question and remained the standard scheme of all naval aircraft until 1935, when the following paints replaced those that had previously been used as standard colours: Dr Kurt Herberts (DKH) L 40/52 *Grau*, or Avionorm-Nitro paint 7375 *Grau* matt, or RLM 02 *Grau*. While there were three choices of grey available, they were theoretically all made to the same standard.

Floats of the aircraft, however, still retained the RLM 01 *Silber* finish for purely chemical reasons; the silver-coloured paint used on areas in contact with water contained aluminium bronze as a colouring pigment, which provided a natural protection against corrosion.

In terms of markings for the aircraft, at this early stage of rearmament, naval aircraft still carried the standard civil registration as described above. However, on 6 July 1933 the *Reichsluftfahrtministerium* (Reich Air Ministry) stipulated that all new aircraft, including seaplanes, were to receive a new form of tail marking. These new tail markings were to consist of three horizontal bands in the black, white, and red of the German flag, with black being the uppermost band, applied to the starboard side of the tail fin across both the fin and rudder. Each of these three coloured bands was to be of the same height, so that each coloured band was exactly one-third of the total height of the combined three-band tail marking. Supplementing this blandishment of nationalism, a single red band overlaid with a central white disc housing a black swastika was increasingly applied to the port side of the tail fin. This practice was not, however, officially adopted until 15 September 1935. It was on this day that the Air Ministry redefined the regulations concerning tail fin markings, now requiring all new aircraft and every aircraft in military service to apply the swastika

Wearing the distinct tri-colour on the vertical stabiliser, these He 59s are part of an unknown training establishment.

band to both sides of the tail fin, thereby replacing the tri-colour band on the starboard side of the aircraft.

Due to the astonishing pace of rearmament, the German military now found itself with an increasing array of aircraft spread across German territory. While this military capacity was initially limited, each passing month brought an increased burden to the organisational control of military aircraft within German territory. To compensate, on 1 April 1934, the Air Ministry divided German territory into six distinct territorial zones, to which fifteen *Luftamter* (air offices) were subordinated. Ostensibly, the formation of these zones had been to regulate and coordinate civil air traffic over German territories. The actual reason for the divisions was in fact to designate territorial areas of command and responsibility for the then still-secret army and naval air forces of Germany. These new territorial commands, known as *Luftkreiskommando* (regional air commands), had as their headquarter cities and commanders:

A poor quality shot of sections of He 60 taking off with the red banded tail visible.

Luftkreiskommando I	Königsberg	*Gen. Lt* Wachenfeld
Luftkreiskommando II	Berlin	*Gen. Lt* Kaupisch
Luftkreiskommando III	Dresden	*Gen. Maj.* Schweickhardt
Luftkreiskommando IV	Münster	*Gen. Lt* Halm
Luftkreiskommando V	München	*Gen. Lt* Eberth
Luftkreiskommando VI	Kiel	*Konteradmiral* Zander

The initial appointment of the previous head of *Gruppe* LS *Konteradmiral* Zander to head *Luftkreiskommando* VI was a reflection of its geographical positioning along Germany's northern coastline. With so much maritime activity in the region, and as a result air and naval interaction, the appointment of Zander was recognition of the primarily naval orientation of the region and its military usefulness and pre-occupation. At the same time, Zander's appointment facilitated a smoother inter-service cooperation between the fledgling German Air Force, the German Navy, and its still small-scale naval aviation programme. The follow-on effect from this arrangement also filtered down to air-sea rescue duties in the Baltic and North Sea and the increasing role aircraft – both civil and military – played in this vital undertaking.

With this reorganisation of Germany, it became apparent that the old style of aircraft registration was no longer adequate. Therefore, a new form of registration was adopted by all military aircraft. This new form of markings now comprised of a five digit code: two numbers, a letter, and two further numbers. Each character in this new form of registration denoted a military-particular specific to an individual aircraft. The first number, read from left to right on the fuselage of an aircraft, signified the *Luftkreis* to which a unit was attached, while the second number identified the aircraft's primary role. The sole letter in the code was the aircraft's unique identification, while the remaining two numbers of the code identified first the *Gruppe* to which the aircraft belong and finally the *Staffel* within that *Gruppe*. As an example, the code '60+A51' could be broken down as follows:

6 – Designation for *Luftkreiskommando* VI
0 – Designation for naval reconnaissance units
A – Individual aircraft letter
5 – The II.*Gruppe*
2 – The 2 *Staffel*

These markings would thus represent the aircraft, 'A', of the 2 *Staffel* of *Küstenfliegergruppe* 506.

Although the presence of a '0' in the registration denoted a naval

A pre-war formation of Heinkel He 60s of 1./506 in flight.

Heinkel He 60s of *Flugzeugführerschule (See)* Warnemünde in July 1938.

reconnaissance unit, it did so only in conjunction with the numeral '6', indicating *Luftkreiskommando* VI. While the other *Luftkreiskommandos* applied the '0' to some of their aircraft, it was done so only to denote an autonomous *Gruppe*, more often than not a reconnaissance unit.

This new form of registration not only applied to front line combat aircraft. It was also applied to aircraft of the training units within each *Luftkreis*. Following the same principles laid out above, the training units of each *Luftkreis* adopted a system comprising of the letter 'S' (indicating a '*Schule*' – school – unit), a number indicating a *Luftkreiskommando*, a letter indicating the aircraft's identity within the school, and a two or three digit number identifying the individual school. Thus seaplane number 48 from *Luftkreiskommando* VI, *Flugzeugführerschule* (*See*) based at Warnemünde would have worn the code, 'S6+B48'.

It was at this time also that the *Balkenkreuz* first appeared on German military aircraft. Similar in design to the black and white crosses displayed on the fuselage of First World War German aircraft, the use of the *Balkenkreuz* was to continue until the fall of the Third Reich in May 1945, albeit with minor variations, but always in the same location on the aircraft. Displayed on both the upper and lower surfaces of the wings as well as the fuselage, the *Balkenkreuz* was an ever-present marking found on German naval aircraft operated under the command of the German military.

The only other form of markings that naval aircraft began adopting around this period were various unit crests and heralds. While many *Jagd-*, *Kampf-* and *Sturzkampfgeschwader* were given the names of various German military and political luminaries, this practice was not extended to German naval air units. Usually only applied on one side of the aircraft, the particular location of the unit's crest depended on the type of aircraft that was operated. For instance, naval units operating the Dornier Do 18 flying boat often applied the *Gruppe*'s crest on the nose, but replicated the aircraft's individual letter on the centreline engine mount; for those units that operated the Heinkel He 59, 60, 114, and 115 seaplanes, the *Staffel* emblem was more often than not to be found on the nose of the aircraft. However, the application of these unit emblems often lay at the discretion of the *Gruppen Kommandeure* and the time and availability of personnel to add them. Indeed, the side to which the unit's crest was applied often varied from *Staffel* to *Staffel*. At times, it was applied to both sides of the aircraft. For special occasions aircraft were uniquely decorated, but the practice was limited.

In 1936, Adolf Hitler announced the formation of a German military air contingent to aid General Franco in the Spanish Civil War. Included within this formation was a small detachment of seaplanes, known as

Above and below: Two unusual photographs showing a Dornier Do 18 of 2./506 painted with a shark's mouth motif. The purpose of this adornment, the duration for which the aircraft retained it and when the photograph was taken is unknown.

Aufklärungsstaffel See 88, or A/S 88 for short. First deployed to Spain in October 1936, the unit comprised of just two each of the He 59 and He 60 seaplane types. Initially, these aircraft were to operate from Cadiz in defence of German and Nationalist shipping ferrying in supplies, troops, and support personnel. However, before the aircraft reached the region, any emblems and markings linking the aircraft to Nazi Germany were removed. Instead, a new scheme of markings was applied, which consisted of a cross motif consistent with that found on all Nationalist aircraft of the time. This symbol was generally to be found on the upper and lower surfaces of the wings, close to the tips, and on the rudder of the aircraft. Supplementing this motif, towards the rear of the fuselage on both sides, just forward of the tailplane, a black roundel was applied in place of the *Balkenkreuz,* with a second also applied below the cockpit, forward of the lower wing's leading edge. Photographic evidence of a death's head motif, super-imposed over the forward roundel on He 59s and the lone Ju 52/3m (W), also exists. However, when these markings were discarded is not known.

In addition to these markings, the aircraft of the unit also wore serial numbers on the fuselage of their aircraft. From October 1936 onwards, the He 60s carried the designation of '51', signifying the aircraft type as a seaplane, followed by a single number representing the aircraft's own number. The first three such He 60s to arrive in Spain were christened *The Terror of the Seas* (511), *The Sea Beast* (512), and *The Sea Wolf* (513). Meanwhile, those He 59s sent to Spain were provided the type number '52'. In February 1937, these designations were changed and the He 60s were re-type numbered as '60' (reconnaissance seaplanes), while the He 59s were re-typed as '71' (bombers).

Although it is possible the aircraft retained their all over RLM 02 *Grau,* an overall colouring of RLM 63, which had become part of the new camouflage system introduced in 1936, may have been applied. This of course depended upon an aircraft's build date. Nominally, aircraft were not repainted before their 1,500 hour/2 year cycle, so given the close proximity of both chroma and tonal value in photographs for RLM 63 and 02, the period is considerably contentious. Furthermore, the 1938 reversion to making 02 standard makes positively identifying the RLM colour that any seaplane was painted exceedingly difficult. The only area not covered in either RLM 63 or 02 was the rudder, which was painted white. Thus, the seaplanes of A/S 88 served with only two officially sanctioned identification markers: the black cross and black roundel. However, as the war progressed A/S 88 adopted its own unofficial emblem, as did most German air units operating in Spain. For the seaplanes of A/S 88, this unofficial emblem was in the form of the ace of spades playing

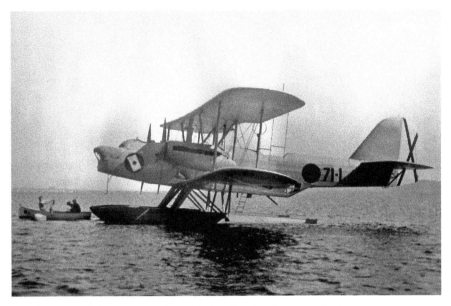

Heinkel 59 coded 71-1 in service with the Condor Legion in Spain.

card superimposed over a black roundel painted on the forward nose on both sides of the aircraft. Tilted forward, the playing card had in the top left corner 'AS', while the diagonal corner had '88'. In addition to these markings, a photograph of an He 59B-2 at Pollensa in 1937 shows the tactical markings of 71-1 in black stencil. Further images of aircraft carrying tactical numbers exist, but evidence also exists of aircraft denuded of such tactical numbering. The last marking applied to the aircraft of A/S 88 appears to have been that of a rearward-pointing white pendant with two small dots, running horizontally, located aft of the fuselage roundel. Pictured in 1937, it is not known whether these markings were a one off, or were employed throughout the career of the unit, as no similar markings have yet been found on non-A/S 88 naval aircraft operating during this time period within Germany.

Back in Germany, at the end of 1938 the draft for instruction L.Dv 521/1 indicated that a top coat of RLM 04 *Gelb* (yellow) for the upper surfaces of seaplanes was to be included in the now-standard RLM 02 finish of naval aircraft. While this application seemed only to be for training aircraft as a visual marker, it was a marking process that was used right up until November 1941 – or at least intended so – when L.Dv 521/1 instructed, 'Shade 04 for naval aircraft camouflage has been abandoned.' Obviously field operators anticipated this instruction, as no such colour has ever been sighted on any naval aircraft after the war started – and for good reason!

In May 1939, the RLM issued a new instruction that saw the

introduction of a new camouflage scheme, replacing the all-over *grau* finish was a tri-colour pattern. The new camouflage scheme featured RLM 72 and 73– two shades of *grün* (green) in a standard splinter pattern on the upper surfaces, while the underside of aircraft received a coat of RLM 65 *hellblau* (light blue). Initially, this new camouflage scheme was applied only to Ar 196 floatplanes, yet by September 1939 all seaplanes and flying boats of combat units – including the returning aircraft of A/S 88 – had been repainted. At this stage, maritime aircraft in training units were not converted to the new camouflage scheme, instead retaining the all-over *grau* finish. This new camouflage scheme was retained by maritime aircraft until the end of the war, the only exception being the application of 7126.21 temporary white for those operating amongst the ice flows of the far north.

This change in appearance for maritime aircraft was part of a raft of changes that swept through the German air forces during 1939. In February of that year, the regional *Luftkreiskommandos* were disbanded and replaced by much larger identities covering greater areas of German territory. These new command units were termed *Luftflotten* (air fleets) and in total four of these new commands were created. With no further use for military codes that identified now defunct parent *Luftkreiskommandos*, on 24 October 1939 all military aircraft officially dropped the five-character code system in preference for a more compact four-character code. The only exception to this was the single-engine fighter units, which although dropping the five-character system, had already begun replacing it with a more refined system of symbols and numbers.

For the seven surviving *Küstenfliegergruppen*, the new unit codes that were issued as a result of these changes were as follows:

KüFlGr. 106	M2
KüFlGr. 306	K6[4]
KüFlGr. 406	K6
KüFlGr. 506	M7, later S4
KüFlGr. 606	8L, later 7T
KüFlGr. 706	6I
KüFlGr. 806	M7

This new form of unit identification was supplemented by two further characters aft of the fuselage *Balkenkreuz*. The first of these two characters was a letter indicating the aircraft, while the second letter indicated the *Staffel* within the *Gruppe* that the aircraft belonged to. Thus, M7+AH was aircraft 'A' of the 1 *Staffel* of *Küstenfliegergruppe* 806.

While every effort was made to keep aircraft markings up to date,

A Heinkel He 114 of 1./Bordfliegergruppe 196 in for maintenance.

often aircraft were temporarily assigned to other *Gruppen* for various operational reasons. In addition, when an aircraft was returned to the factory for major repairs or overhaul, that aircraft was not always returned to its original unit. Under operational conditions, the re-coding of aircraft was often not a priority, so several aircraft survived in *Staffeln* with codes belonging to a different unit entirely. In some case, these aircraft retained their codes long enough to acquire their own bestowed personalities and status within units, and thus their unique codes were left unchanged.

Interestingly, aircraft often retained the final part of its *Stammkennzeichen*, or factory code, mixed with only the *Verbandkennzeichen* added. An example of this was M2+YK, which was shot down on 26 September 1939 over the North Sea. Originally built in 1938 by the Dornier factory in Friedrichshafen, the flying boat had been given the factory codes KY+YK. After the aircraft was taken on strength by 2./506, the aircraft only had the *Verbändkennzeichen* of KüFlGr 506 in use at the time applied (M7), leaving the latter two letters of the *Stammkennzeichen* in place as both the aircraft and *Staffel* letters. This practice of mixing *Stamm-* and *Verbändkennzeichen* appears to have been a widespread, if not standard, practice at least during the early days of the war, often making positive identification of aircraft and parent units difficult.

Applied in the same position as the *Verbändkennzeichen*, a *Stammkennzeichen* was simply a four-letter code applied to an aircraft during its manufacture. These codes were used specifically as the aircraft's air traffic control identification during transit between bases, remaining the normal identification call sign for all air traffic procedures throughout the life of the aircraft. In addition, the *Stammkenzeichen* aided the RLM in its procurement programmes.

While the practice of emblem application was mostly standard, the addition of personal motifs or slogans on aircraft was relatively rare. Although several aircraft did receive such anthropomorphic devices and crew members did scrawl personal markings near their stations, the practice of nose art was not nearly as widespread among *Küstenfliegergruppen* as in the Allied air forces.

In October 1939, there was a general reorganisation of all *Küstenfliegergruppen* and the activation of a new unit. This new unit, KüFlGr 906, was given the *Verbändkennzeichen* 8L. As most of its aircraft were sourced from other units, KüFlGr 906 operated its seaplanes and flying boats well into the winter of 1939 more often than not still wearing the *Verbändkennzeichen* of the units from which each aircraft had come. Similarly, in August 1943, when *Küstenfliegerstaffel Krim* was activated on the Russian Front, it was assigned the *Verbändkennzeichen* 6M (later 1K), yet the majority of its aircraft retained the previous identification, their *Stammkennziechen*.

Unlike the majority of other German air units, the camouflage and markings of *Küstenflieger* units remained relatively stable throughout their operation. Even when the *Küstenfliegergruppen* were dissolved and its aircraft transferred or absorbed into other seaplane units, the aircraft's camouflage system was retained with minimal, if any, changes. The only addition was temporary snow camouflage for those aircraft operating in the Arctic region.

4

Küstenfliegergruppe 106

As part of the reorganisation of German air units, on 1 October 1936 the three *Staffeln* of *Fliegergruppe (See)* 106 were renamed as *Küstenfliegergruppe* 106. In doing so, the *Gruppe* became the first *Küstenfliegergruppe* in the German order of battle. In addition to this, the *Gruppe* was furnished with a *Stabsstaffel,* which was activated the same day. In command of the new unit was *Oberstleutnant* Ulrich Kessler, while *Major* Walter Weygoldt acted as the *Gruppe*'s *Major beim Stabe* (later promoted to *Staffelkapitän* of 2./106 on 1 May 1937). As with all *Küstenfliegergruppen* at the time, the development and expansion process was a prolonged one. The growth of the maritime aviation branch of the *Wehrmacht* meant the availability of spare parts and equipment was slow in reaching front line units. Despite this, the crews of the newly named unit had a variety of activities that kept them busy; everything from lectures on weapons maintenance and operational procedures, emergency drills, formation flying, and regular exercise were all part of daily life. Early officers of the new *Gruppe* included *Obstlt* Hans-Arnim Czech (*Staffelkapitän* of 3./106), *Hptm* Wolfgang Bühring (*Staffelkapitän* of 1./106), *Hptm* Günter Klünder, *Hptm* Wilhelm Kern, *Oblt* Edgar Ceasar, *Oblt* Arno Kleyenstüber, *Lt.z.S* Günther-Paul Krech, *Lt.z.S* Ernst-Heinrich Thomsen, and *Lt* Gert Müller-Trimbusch.

With the German presence in Spain on the increase, many of the *Gruppe*'s members found themselves transferred there for service with *Aufklärungsstaffel (See)* 88 on short-service rotation. The experience gained under operational conditions there proved a boost to the *Gruppe*'s efficiency. As with all *Küstenfliegergruppen* of the time, the unit was equipped with the He 60 short-range reconnaissance aircraft, the long-range Do 18 flying boat, and the multipurpose He 59 seaplane for the 1,

A pre-war photograph of a Do 18 of 2./106 in flight on a clear day in 1938.

The pre-war flight line of 3./106 He 59s whilst stationed at Borkum during April 1939.

2, and 3 *Staffel* respectively. By the end of August 1939, only the 3 *Staffel* was not based at Norderney, it being located at Borkum.

War

With the outbreak of hostilities in September 1939, the *Gruppe* found itself employed in the reconnaissance of the North Sea, Kattegat, and Skagerrak. The focus was two-fold: orders were to locate any Polish shipping attempting to flee westward, while general reconnaissance was necessary to ascertain British shipping movements and any possible attempts at reinforcing the beleaguered Polish forces. To achieve this, each *Staffeln* was up to strength and supported by *Hptm* Stein's 3./706, which had been subordinated to *Stab./*106. On 1 September, a general alert had been telexed to all *Staffeln* to maintain a 1-hour readiness. While the alert amounted to nothing, by 4 September the unit was engaged in widespread reconnaissance operations. Standing orders henceforth made it clear that, 'All enemy submarines spotted inside the mission area must be engaged and destroyed.' A further stipulation noted that reconnaissance was to focus on locating and identifying all objects seen floating on the surface of the sea. The *Kriegsmarine* was particularly concerned about the potential for minefields to be sown in the German Bight and the entrance to the Skagerrak and the risk it would pose to their operations and the German merchant fleet. However, during September little surface activity was noted.

First Losses, First Kills

The opening day of the war with Britain was disastrous for 2./106. Ordered to undertake reconnaissance in the North Sea for British naval forces attempting to reinforce Poland on 3 September, Do 18 M2+JK (WNr 0723) crashed during the operation, killing all on board. The four-man crew comprised of *Oblt.d.Res* Georg Neckargemünd (B), *Uffz* Friedrich Minden (F), *Uffz* Martin Maltach (Bf), and *Uffz* Ludwig Utzmeir (Bm). The loss was soon compensated for, yet the early casualties did not bode well for the unit. Two days later, at 05:25 hours on 5 September, Avro Anson 'B' (K6183) of 206 Squadron took off on a routine patrol of the North Sea. At around the same time, eight He 115s of 1./106 took off from Norderney on a similar operation. Midway through the patrol, M2+FH encountered the Anson, whereupon a dogfight ensued. After an aerial battle lasting some 15 minutes, the Anson eventually exploded when the German crew scored hits on the wings of the Avro, setting its fuel tanks alight. Only the pilot, Flt Off. Edwards was saved when the German crew alighted on the water and pulled him from the frigid waters. Almost a week later, it would be the Germans turn to loose a patrol aircraft over the North Sea.

On the evening of 11 September, 2./106 was alerted for a patrol the following morning over the western fringes of the North Sea. Taking off as part of a six-strong reconnaissance patrol, the crew of M2+EK (WNr 0717) suffered technical difficulties on the return leg and were forced to make an emergency landing on the sea at 10:20 hours. Radioing their situation, a second aircraft of the *Staffel* on patrol nearby quickly located the crew and began circling the landing sight. Also on patrol nearby was the U-boat U-13, which had left Wilhemshaven the day before on its third patrol of the war. Under the command of *Kapitänleutnant* Karl Daublebsky von Eichhain, U-13 altered course to take aboard the stranded flyers, while the flying boat was located and taken under tow by the support ship *Günther Plüschow*. However, at 12:20 hours the following day the aircraft capsized and sank. While the loss highlighted the dangers inherent in operations over water, the quick rescue of the crew did much to help morale within the *Staffel*. Yet the report of missing aircrew would soon become a reality.

On 12 September, six aircraft from 1./106 had been detailed for a reconnaissance operation. At 14:21 hours, one of the six He 115s (M2+LH) was engaged by a Dutch Fokker seaplane. Later investigations noted that the Dutch aircraft had come out of the sun and surprised the Germans who responded with a 'shoot-first-ask-questions-later' mentality. The Dutch pilot attempted an emergency landing on the sea, but his aircraft overturned in the swell. Immediately, the Germans landed nearby to rescue the stranded Dutchmen before returning them to Norderney. Of the Dutch crew, two men suffered light skin abrasions, one a bruised shoulder and neck abrasions, while another had been shot in the toe. During the short combat and subsequent rescue operation, M2+LK (WNr 0178) of 2./106 attempted to alight on the water near the stricken Dutch machine, but in doing so suffered some damage that precluded it from taking off again. As a result, the German crew was forced to taxi the aircraft along the surface of the water and beach it at Ameland, where *Lt.z.S.* Horst Rust (B), *Fw.* Radons (F), *Fk.Mt.* Zieschang (h.B), and *Uffz.* Schenk (Bm) were all interned.

Throughout the remainder of September, October, and into November, the main focus of reconnaissance for the *Gruppe* was between 52° and 55° N and from the British coastline to 5° E. Despite this focus, operations were still conducted in and around the German Bight and the Skagerrak, where a close eye was kept on shipping movements. The reorganisation of maritime units in October 1939 did not impact the *Gruppe*, and so its

Above and below: Reconnaissance operations over the North Sea required aircrew to fly close to vessels to identify the nationality and potential cargo of any shipping encountered. Here a Dornier crew flies low over a German vessel close in shore.

ability to function in a cohesive manner was not interrupted. However, intermittent losses still hampered the *Gruppe*; On 8 November, *Uffz* Grabbe (F), *Lt.z.S* Boettger (B), and *Fk.Mt* Schettler (h.B) of 1./106 were posted as 'missing in action' after failing to return from patrol, while on 29 November the *Gruppe* suffered its single heaviest day of losses.

Starting with the collision of two Do 18 of 2./106 (M2+DK -WNr. 722 and M2+HK - WNr. 842) during takeoff at 07:05 hours, a further five Dornier's were lost in combat during the day while engaged in mining operations. The aircraft involved from 1./106 were K6+FH (WNr. 738) and K6+KH (WNr. 830), while 2./106 lost K6+DK (WNr. 724), K6+GK (WNr. 787), and K6+FK (WNr. 707). In total, the *Gruppe* lost twenty airmen, four of whom were killed. These losses represented 41 per cent of operational Dornier flying boats then available for combat within the *Gruppe*. Obviously, such losses were unsustainable and prompted the Germans to lament, 'This has been a black day for the *Luftstreitkräfte*.' Three of the flying boats had been intercepted and shot down by Coastal Command aircraft, while an accident, an engine failure, and lack of fuel accounted for the others. These losses were further added to when on the morning of 7 December, *Oblt.z.S* Giesbert Clemens and his 3./106 crew were killed when He 59 M2+OL (Wnr 1974) crashed on landing after a mining operation. The cost in aircraft and crews that mining operations

The *Luftwaffe* and *Kriegsmarine* personnel of 2./106 in front of a *Staffel* Dornier flying boat.

represented led the German staff to temporarily halt such operations until a more suitable aircraft could be found to undertake the hazardous work.

Despite the losses, the *Gruppe*'s efficiency remained high, particularly that of the 2 *Staffel*. Between the start of the war in September and New Year's Eve, 2./106 flew 239,970 km in 1,263 hours of flight. This figure would be supplemented with a further 83 hours of flight during January 1940, which covered 9,570 km. The drop in operational flying during January was a reflection of the poor weather conditions, which closed many of the North Sea seaplane bases, although losses and a lack of replacements did not help matters either.

War Against the Royal Navy

As a regular practice, the various *Staffeln* of the *Gruppe* undertook routine searches in a fan-like pattern. Taking off from their respective bases, individual aircraft would fly their patrol lines in radiating, but parallel formations. This method allowed the greatest possible search area to be covered, while providing an element of mutual support for individual aircraft. On 21 October, such an operation was undertaken by six aircraft of 1./106. At about 10:30 hours, the crew of M2+IH – *Lt.z.S* Happe (B), *Uffz* Müller (F), *Uffz* Gornetzki (h.B) – spotted six English destroyers in line-ahead formation. As Happe later recorded:

> Due to prevailing cloud cover, I was able to descend to 800 m. The destroyers opened fire on me. The chance for a bomb run on the destroyers was not possible due to the weather and the element of surprise having been lost. I circled the destroyers for 15 minutes. There was also a cruiser in the vicinity, but due to fuel shortages I was forced to return to base.

Happe landed at Norderney at 12.21 p.m.

In the meantime, Happe signalled his discovery. Shortly thereafter, the crew of M2+AH, comprising *Hptm* von Schrötter (B), *Ofw* Botterbrote (F), and *Fw* Freitag (h.B), arrived. At around 11:22 hours, the crew sighted shipping that was immediately identified as hostile destroyers. While observing the enemy fleet in order to assess course and type, Schrötter witnessed a second aircraft [M2+IH] ahead off the stern destroyer, which was firing upon it. Like Happe and his crew, von Shrötter's attempts at an attack were foiled for similar reasons. Von Schrötter later reported that any attack on the vessels was impossible:

A surprise attack was no longer possible, as the flak defences started immediately and any attack by a single aircraft was impossible. The visibility was so good that every prepared attack would be recognised immediately and a defence mounted. Given an attack approach time of 3 minutes, such intense defences would be impossible to breach, while a high attack offered the same outlooks, because at 1,200 m there was a closed cloud layer. Also, the same defences could target a high flying aircraft and a single bomb run aimed with the Lotfe bomb sight were decreased with regard to hit possibility.

The inability to target well-defended targets of opportunity was a concern, but on 7 November *Lt.z.S* Happe and his crew were able to make an attack. Operating as part of a fan-search in M2+IH, Happe noted an English destroyer about 25 miles off the coast of Felixstowe. Flying a circuit around the ship, the crew noticed a submarine close by the destroyer, with a second a little farther away. After identifying the submarine as definitely British, Happe ordered an attack.

The defensive AA barrage meant Happe needed two attempts before finally being able to drop a brace of SC250 bombs on his third attack. Happe observed:

> The first two bombs landed about 40 m from the submarine, and the third only 10 m away. Due to the fusing, this bomb exploded about 15-20 m from the boat. After releasing the bombs, a curved track to port was flown in order to assess the effect of the attack. At the end of this track, I noted the submarine was half submerged. By the time we returned to the bomb sight, the boat was already submerged. A large oily patch was noted on the surface where the boat had submerged. Due to failing weather, we could not stay in the area much longer and we had already lost sight of the destroyer. At 10:35 we abandoned our patrol.

The submarine in question was most likely HMS *Seal*, which was to rendezvous with the destroyer HMS *Boadicea*. The destroyer was to act as an escort for *Seal* and two other submarines – L26 and *Cachalot* – on their return to Portsmouth. HMS *Seal* reported being attacked by a seaplane that dropped three bombs at 10:35 hours in the approximate position 52°00′ N 02°05′ E. Neither L26 nor *Cachalot* was attacked, and the *Seal* reported it sustained no damage.

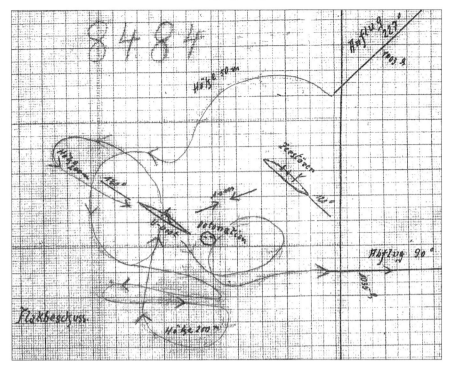

The hand-drawn attack plan flown by *Lt.z.S* Happe on 7 November 1939 against the English submarine HMS *Seal*. The British submarine would again be attacked by *Küstenflieger* aircraft in 1940.

1940 and Scandinavia

The winter of 1939/40 proved a rather severe one. As a result, operations were restricted, with many of the seaplane harbours becoming unserviceable due to ice forming on the sea. Consequently, the *Gruppe*'s contribution to the war at sea remained limited. Despite this, losses continued to mount. On 28 March 1940, Do 18 M2+GK failed to return from a sortie over the North Sea. The crew of *Fw* Wilhelm Harms (F), *Lt.z.S* Karl Bölk (B), *Fk.Mt.* Werner Lenzen (h.B), and *Uffz* Kasimir Niezgotka (Bm) were all listed as missing in action.

With the spring thaw came a new operation designed to protect Germany's northern flank. *Unternehmen Weserübung* (Operation Weser Exercise) was designed to capture Denmark and Norway and thereby prevent any Allied incursions from the north. The operation was launched in the early hours of 9 April 1940. For the 1 *Staffel*, this meant a move to the captured Norwegian base at the town of Stavanger on the afternoon of the invasion. While German forces gained complete surprise, operations in the north of the country were soon in difficulty. As a result, the Germans began to expect Allied counter-attacks, which came in the form of a Royal Navy sortie to Narvik.

In charge of naval forces at Narvik, which comprised ten destroyers of the 1934A and 1936 class (Georg Thiele, Wolfgang Zenker, Bernd von Arnim, Erich Giese, Erich Koellner, Diether von Roeder, Hans Lüdemann, Hermann Künne, Wilhelm Heidkamp, and Anton Schmitt), was *Konteradmiral* Friedrich Bonte. The plan had been for the destroyers to refuel in Narvik before returning to Germany. However, the loss of one of the supply tankers en route meant Bonte was unable to refuel quickly enough before the Royal Navy launched a counter-attack. At dawn the following day, Captain Warburton-Lee, the commander of the British 2nd Destroyer Flotilla, slipped into Narvik Bay with five H-Class destroyers (HMS *Hardy, Hotspur, Havick, Hostile,* and *Hunter*). In the ensuing battle, Wilhelm Heidkamp and Anton Schmitt were sunk, while Diether von Roeder was heavily damaged. Although HMS *Hardy* and *Hunter* were sunk and HMS *Hotspur* damaged, the raid sent alarm bells ringing through the German High Command.

Any attempt to send air-support north would strain the already over-burdened and fuel-strapped forces at Narvik, as German aircraft would need to land and refuel before attempting a return journey. By 13 April, the situation had become critical in the North. The British had launched

Dornier Do 18 60+C52 undergoes pre-flight checks at Hörnum. Clearly visible is the *Staffel's* emblem. Of note is the summer peak on the NCO's cap.

a second sortie to Narvik, this time supported by the battleship HMS *Warspite*. In desperate need of air support, four He 115 of 1./106 sortied to Narvik from Stavanger, where they found the *Warspite*. However, their attempts at attacking the battleship were driven off due to heavy AA fire. Withdrawing, the four aircraft found and unsuccessfully attacked the British destroyer HMS *Ivanhoe*. Short on fuel, the four aircraft landed at Narvik, where they spent the night. The following day, the formation set out for Stavanger, but as they overflew Vestfjord on their return, they were engaged by British warships, which shot down *Lt.z.S* Joachim Vogler (B) and his crew. While Vogler was killed, *Uffz* Ernst Welp (F), *Uffz* Karl Caiser (Bf), and *OGfr* Walter Hinstedt (Bm) were captured. Meanwhile, He 115 (WNr 2400), with *Oblt.z.S* Hermann Bärmer (B), *Oblt* Hans Hattenbach (F), *Ofw* Wilhelm Pfau (Bf), and Heinrich Stripper (Bm), was captured when forced to ditch due to damage south of Vega Island.

Losses in Norway continued to mount for the *Staffel*. On 17 April, four He 115s were destroyed (Wnr 1878, 1879, 1898, and 2087) when the British cruiser HMS *Suffolk* shelled Stavanger for 80 minutes during the morning. As the British ship withdrew, the *Luftwaffe* launched a massive search for the *Suffolk*. Included in this were Do 18s of 2./106 based at Rantum, and it was M2+KK that made the first sighting, enabling land-based units to begin their assault on the ship.

An early war photograph of a 3 *Staffel* Heinkel He 59 being craned into the water ready for an operation. Of interest are the large underwing markings visible on the aircraft. By the time of the Norwegian campaign, the *Staffel* had converted to the Heinkel He 115.

Meanwhile, in Narvik the situation continued to deteriorate. Orders were issued for 1./106 to send three relief sorties to the beleaguered troops in the port. However, in atrocious weather conditions the formation was forced to turn back. Unfortunately, *Oblt.z.S* Witt and his crew were killed when their aircraft crashed near Vosna Island, west of Trondheim.

Meanwhile, operations for the 2 and 3 *Staffeln* continued farther south. The majority of operations undertaken were reconnaissance patrols of the North Sea and anti-submarine operations in the Skagerrak. By early May, Southern Norway had been secured, but resistance in the north and a British counter-landing at Namsos continued to worry the Germans. With the invasion of France on 10 May 1940, the focus again shifted back to Europe. The same day, 2./106 had sent out a reconnaissance operation to locate the British Task Force RZ (centred around the cruiser HMS *Birmingham*). Covering the ships was a screen of Hudsons, which engaged Do 18 M2+EK after it located the task force. In the subsequent melee, the Dornier was forced down after suffering heavy damage. Thankfully, the sea was relatively calm and their distress calls were heard by the crew of M2+HK, which arrived on the scene a short time later. After setting M2+EK alight, the crew of the two flying boats departed the scene and returned to Rantum. By the end of June 1940, operations in Norway had been completed successfully and the *Gruppe* was able to focus again on the western side of the North Sea and its role in supporting the war against British trade.

War Against Britain

The intensification of war against Britain in the summer of 1940 placed increasing demands on the *Luftwaffe*. Consequently, there arose a dispute between Göring and Raeder in late June and early July about the transfer of naval air units to *Luftwaffe* control. As part of Göring's desire to crush Britain and gain control of all air units, he requested the transfer of 3./106 to his control. Raeder flatly objected to the request on the grounds that the improved strategic situation afforded by the capture of the Atlantic Coast and Norway meant his U-boat force needed support from a naval-controlled air arm more than ever. While Göring acquiesced, it was not the last time he cast covetous eyes on the *Gruppe*.

With the successful conclusion of the French campaign in June, 1./106 was transferred to Brest to provide reconnaissance capabilities in the region. This was further supplemented on 23 July with the transfer of 2./106 to Brest as it made its redeployment to Cherbourg the following month. In addition to 3./106, then based at Schellingwoude in northern Holland, the

Gruppe continued to operate against British trade. Although the supply of aerial mines remained limited, the 1 and 3 *Staffeln* often participated in operations to sow mines along the British coastline and in harbour areas. Meanwhile, the Do 18-equipped 2./106 flew reconnaissance operations over the Cornish coast and out into the Celtic Sea. These operations proved hazardous so close to British air bases. On 25 September 1940, *Oblt.z.S* Stelle (B), *Oblt* Heuveldop (F), *Fw* Brasch (Bf), and *Uffz* Kahlfeld (Bm) were lost when Do 18 M2+EK (WNr 393) was intercepted over the St George's Channel by Plt Off. Russell of 236 Squadron while he was on patrol in his Blenheim. While Heuveldop was able to successfully ditch his stricken Dornier and the crew are known to have taken to their life-raft, no further trace of all but Stelle was ever found. On 26 October, the body of Hans-Dietrich Stelle was washed ashore at Church Cove, east of Lizard Rock.

By the time Stelle's body had washed ashore, changes were underway within the group. In early October, 3./106 was alerted that it was to transfer to Barth where it was to undertake a conversion course to the Junkers Ju 88. The ominous order heralded that the unit was shortly destined for *Luftwaffe* control. The change-over in aircraft type by 3./106 was closely followed by more changes.

A familiar sight with the Dorniers; an unidentified 2 *Staffel* machine is aided by a German vessel after suffering technical difficulties. The crew are securing the inflatable dinghy on the wing while another member covers the observer's forward hatch with a canvas cover to prevent the aircraft being swamped whilst undertow.

Above and below: Two photographs of the facilities along the French coast taken in late 1940 by a Dornier crew returning after an operational sortie to St George's Channel.

On 29 November 1940, there was a revision to the unit designations. To maintain operational consistency on that day, 2./106 was redesignated as the 3 *Staffel* of *Küstenfliegergruppe* 906. Immediately, the unit was reformed at Barth, and like the 3 *Staffel* began working up on the Ju 88. While 3./106 had recommenced operations, this left the He 115-equipped 1 *Staffel* as the only true maritime unit of the *Gruppe* still on operations. Flying out of Brest-Hourtin, the *Staffel* continued to act as maritime reconnaissance while occasionally undertaking mining operations.

Given the conditions of 1940-1941 were not as severe as those the previous winter, operations during this period continued. However, the change to Ju 88 bombers meant the 2 and 3 *Staffeln* were increasingly used in operations against land-based objectives. With this came an increased risk. On 21 and 22 February, the *Gruppe* lost three crews to various causes. On the first day, the *Staffelkaptiän* of 3./106, *Hptm* Walter Holte, was killed when the Ju 88A-5 (WNr 6184) crashed at Nord-Wickhout after an operational sortie. Killed along with Holte, who was acting as the pilot, were *Fw* Fritz Pötzold (B), *Gfr* Karl Carl (Bf), and *Ofw* Heinrich Mantel (Bs). The following day, two Hurricanes from 111 Squadron intercepted a He 115 while on patrol off Peterhead. The British pilots, Plt Off. Bain and Gregory, claimed the floatplane as a probable. The machine, M2+IH (WNr 2750) of 1./106, had aboard *Ofw* Wilhelm Arheit (F), *Lt.z.S* Theodor Kach (B), and *Fw* Paul Gornetzki (Bf). Only the remains of Arheit were found. Unaware of the situation, the failure of Koch and his crew to return from their sortie prompted the *Staffel* to order *Oblt* Peter Midderhoff (F), *Hptm* Günter Grützmacher (B), and *Fw* Heinz Hark (Bf) to search for the missing aircraft. Inexplicably, the aircraft in which they were flying, M2+AH (WNr 3249), crashed into the sea during the sortie, killing all aboard. The loss of three crews in such a short space of time impacted the *Gruppe*'s efficiency. With an increasing threat to daylight operations, the various *Staffeln* began operating under the cover of darkness. This did little to improve efficiency, although it did somewhat reduce the risks involved. Despite this, on the night of 13/14 March, 3./106 lost yet another crew. Ordered to operate over Glasgow, Ju 88A-5 M2+JL (WNr 2234) was shot down in flames off the coast of Northumberland by Flt Lt Sheen of 72 Squadron. On board, the doomed Junkers were *Oblt* Hildebrand Voigtländer-Tetzner (F), *Lt* Rudolf Dietz (B), *OGfr* Walter Wesserer (Bf), and *OGfr* Hans Vandanne (Bm), none of whom survived.

Küstenflieger

Two views of Heinkel He 115, M2+GH, being prepared for a sortie. Often crews would decorate their armaments with slogans, or as in this case, a shark motif.

Dornier Do 18 M2+EK is worked on by mechanics and crew as it is prepared for hoisting aboard a catapult ship.

Kampfgruppe 106

While operations continued through April 1941, the *Luftwaffe*'s build up of forces in the east and the Balkans necessitated a reinforcing of air strength in the west. To achieve this, during May the final naval air unit of *Küstenfliegergruppe* 106, the 1 *Staffel*, was ordered to Barth to undertake conversion training to the Ju 88. With all three units now operating land-based aircraft, the pretence of maritime operations was finally dispelled, and henceforth the *Gruppe* became known as *Kampfgruppe* 106 and was subordinate to direct control by the *Luftwaffe*. The unit, in its new guise, continued to operate until September 1942, when it formed the nucleus of the II *Gruppe* of *Kampfgeschwader* 6.

5

Küstenfliegergruppe 206

In 1936, German naval air strength stood at three short-range reconnaissance and one long-range reconnaissance *Staffeln*, two *Jagdstaffeln*, and two general purpose *Staffeln*. With the first round of aircraft production complete, the *Kriegsmarine* sought ways to expand its operational capabilities in the air. Naval studies had shown that the intended twenty-five *Staffeln* force originally sought was no longer adequate. This was especially the case if war broke out with Great Britain. Therefore, in 1936 the Naval High Command requested a modified arrangement that increased its air assets to sixty-two *Staffeln*. These new units were to replace the *Fliegergruppen (See)* and were designed to be entirely more naval in appearance and operation.

On 1 July 1936, the three *Staffeln* 2.(M)/*Fliegergruppe (See)* 116, 2.(F)/*Fliegergruppe (See)* 106, and 2.(Mz)/*Fliegergruppe* 106 were all disbanded and immediately reformed as the 1, 2, and 3 *Staffeln* of *Küstenfliegergruppe* 206. Aside from the 1 *Staffel*, which was based at Norderney, the *Gruppe*'s operations were conducted from the seaplane facilities at Kiel-Holtenau.

In keeping with the desired structure of a naval air *Gruppe*, the 1 *Staffel* was a tactical reconnaissance unit designed primarily to operate in support of coastal artillery, spotting, naval, and merchant operations. As a result, the unit was supplied with the He 60. For long-range reconnaissance, the 2 *Staffel* was equipped with the Do 18 flying boat, while the 3 *Staffel*, which functioned as an all-purpose unit, was assigned the He 59 seaplane. Unlike later formed *Küstenfliegergruppen*, the three *Staffeln* of *Küstenfliegergruppe* 206 were subordinated to outside *Stäbe*, as no command unit was ever formed. It also appears that the unit adopted just a single emblem for use on its He 60s only – three dice and gambling cup. Given the increasing number of air units being activated

Heinkel He 60 of 1./206 whilst stationed at Norderney.

An in-flight photograph showing the emblem of 1./206.

in Germany at the time, this lack of identity was unusual, although not uncommon.

As with all naval air units of the time, the main preoccupation of the three *Staffeln* was training and general duties. The obligatory coastal reconnaissance operations were conducted by the He 60s of the 1 *Staffel*. However, a great deal of time was spent on lectures pertaining to operational flying, weather, reconnaissance, and rescue duties, as well as general maintenance and mechanics of the aircraft and their weapons. It was expected that all crew members were to be proficient in basic repairs to aircraft and have at least a workable knowledge of all the systems and their use aboard the aircraft.

In 1937, a second reorganisation of naval air units was undertaken. In order to properly align the various units to their numerical sequenced activation, at the end of June 1937 *Küstenfliegergruppe* 206 was redesignated *Küstenfliegergruppe* 106. No change in any of the three *Staffeln*'s equipment or roles was undertaken; the 1, 2, and 3 *Staffeln* of *Küstenfliegergruppe* 206 merely transposed '106' over their title *Küstenfliegergruppe* instead. Twelve months to the day after it was activated, on 1 July 1937, Küstenfliegergruppe 206 was officially disbanded, never to be reformed.

6
Küstenfliegergruppe 306

Unlike the normal procedure for activating new units within the *Luftwaffe*, *Küstenfliegergruppe* 306 was initially raised without a *Gruppenstab*. Originally, the 1 *Staffel* of the unit had been formed by renaming the 1.(M)/*Fliegergruppe (See)* 106 *Staffel* on 1 July 1936. Like its predecessor, the *Staffel* operated the He 60. From July 1936 until March 1937, when the *Gruppenstab* was raised, the 1 *Staffel* remained the only representative of the proposed new Gruppe. As more aircraft were produced by German industry, the expansion process continued. As a result, on 1 November 1938 a second combat *Staffel*, operating the Dornier 18, was added to the *Gruppe*. Unlike the 1 *Staffel*, the 2 *Staffel* was raised from scratch.

Pre-War Operations

Like many of the pre-war *Küstenfliegergruppen*, the unit was engaged mostly in reconnaissance of German shipping lanes in the Baltic and North Sea. Predominantly, this required aircrew to practise low-level flight and maintain their abilities in identifying the tonnage of shipping, its course, and speed. On rare occasions, the unit sometimes operated in support of any stricken vessel that required assistance while at sea.

The compliment of *Kriegsmarine* personnel that were assigned to the 2 *Staffeln* was no different to that of any other *Küstenfliegerstaffeln*. While those who survived their tour in the air arm eventually returned to the *Kriegsmarine*, they did so in anonymity, with one exception. Born in Hamburg in 1915, Paul Just enlisted in 1936. In 1939, he transferred to the 1./306 as an observer, being awarded the Iron Cross, 2nd Class, and the Observer's Badge in Bronze. In January 1941, Paul transferred

The crew and of 60+K32 stay aboard as their aircraft is winched from the water.

to the *U-bootwaffe*, making his first patrol as the 1 Watch Officer aboard U-156 in September 1941. In June 1943, he was given command of U-546, ultimately making two war patrols totalling 237 days at sea. On 24 April 1945, U-546 was sunk by depth charges from US destroyers in position 43°53′ N 40°07′ W, for the loss of twenty-six sailors. Paul Just was captured and held as a prisoner of war in the Charles Street Gaol in Boston until his release on 12 March 1946.

Wartime Experiences

Prior to the war, the *Luftwaffe* had set up two distinct commands in order to cope with the different requirements of aerial operations over the Baltic and the North Sea regions. As a result, *Fliegerführern der Luftstreitkräfte Ost* and *West* were created to supervise the respective regions.

On 1 September 1939, the *Gruppe* had been subordinate to *F.d.L Ost*.

A 2 *Staffel* machine is prepared for a sortie. Clearly visible is the *Staffel* emblem which was retained when the unit was redesignated 2./106 in July 1937.

However, with the entry of Britain into the war, on 4 September the Stab and the 1./306 were ordered to move to Hörnum, where the former was to take command of the long-range screening reconnaissance operations of the Do 18 equipped 1./306, 2./506, and 2./606. This left the 1 *Staffel*, based at Dievenow, under the command of *Stab./506*, itself based at Pillau.

Throughout September, the 1 *Staffel* received increasing quantities of aircraft so that by 7 October, it had on strength far more than was its usual compliment, including ten He 60s, three He 59s, and eight He 114s. The latter types had been issued as surplus to requirements, however they were still used, albeit sparingly, in the combat role. Although the number of aircraft was on the increase, during early September two He 59s and their crews were transferred from the 1 *Staffel* to supplement the needs of 3./706. The loss of the two aircraft and crews did not seriously hamper operations by the unit.

In the west, 2./306 continued operations as and when serviceability and the weather allowed. For the most part, operations were conducted over the North Sea, with three sorties, each requiring 2,100 litres of fuel, being launched on 9 September to cover the Shetland area. Much of the *Gruppe*'s activity throughout September was hampered by the constant call from *F.d.L. Ost* to transfer He 114s and their crews to Großenbrode for reconnaissance work in the Baltic. However, the experience that the *Gruppe* gained in this endeavour was rewarded on 16 September when 1./306 was selected as a trial unit (along with 1./706) to develop boarding tactics. In an effort to intensify the war on trade, it was decided that the He 59 of the units would carry an extra officer, a radioman, and one or two soldiers that could be sent aboard suspicious ships for the purpose of searching, and if necessary, destroying illicit cargoes. The proposal required the crews of the unit to be instructed in boarding law, which was completed on 28 September. According to the war diary of the *Oberbefehlshaber der Marine,* the following procedure was to be employed during the search process:

> He 59 sends a request to suspicious ship to stop engines and to lower a boat. Ship must be readied for frisk action, all ship's documents must be kept ready. One He 59 stays in the air, while a second lands by the ship, disembarks 'boarding commando' to search the ship or if necessary to take the ship to Swinemünde.

The *Ark Royal* and Her Escape

On 26 September, *Küstenfliegergruppe* 306 was scheduled to launch eighteen reconnaissance sorties during the morning. Unlike most other operations, the day's reconnaissance uncovered a substantial British fleet withdrawing from the North Sea. Between 10:45 and 11:25 hours, the various aircraft of the *Gruppe* observed three task forces, comprised of, as the war diary went on to claim:

> Group A: sector 4699, course of 260°, speed: 20 knots. This flotilla consisted of two battleships, one aircraft carrier, four cruisers (presence of destroyers unlikely). Group B: sector 3440, probably western course, speed unknown. It consisted of two battle cruisers, one aircraft carrier, five destroyers. Group C: sector 4944, consisting of two cruisers, six destroyers, heading for the west at high speed.

The *Gruppe*'s Do 18s stayed in contact for most of the morning, experiencing flak and fighter interception. Given that the enemy ships were now about 250 nautical miles from Heligoland, this did not stop the

The arming points for the time-fused bombs on the wings of a Dornier Do 18. Such small armaments did little in the way of damage to any major ship, but were suitable against smaller vessels.

Luftwaffe from sending nine He 111s of 1./*Kampfgeschwader* 26 and four Ju 88s of I./*Kampfgeschwader* 30, which attacked later that afternoon. Although the attack produced no tangible results, despite what the German propaganda proclaimed, the efforts of the *Küstenfliegergruppen* (1./406 was involved in the reconnaissance also) proved how capable and necessary maritime reconnaissance was. Unfortunately, with the so-claimed sinking of the aircraft carrier HMS *Ark Royal*, the efforts of the *Küstenflieger* were overlooked. The mass of attention *Gefreiter* Carl Francke received for supposedly sinking the *Ark Royal* prompted the Navy to signal various other departments that:

> In contrast to the radio report from the evening of 28.9 announcing that only land-based aircraft took part in the operation [26.9] against enemy naval forces and aircraft carrier, we want to stress the point that the enemy forces were tracked down by flying boats of the *Seekriegsleitung* and then were shadowed for 11 hours by same; of which 4 hours were flown over enemy territory despite flak and fighters. The attack of land-based units would not have been possible without the actions of the seaplanes. We are asking you publish a correction.

Unfortunately for the *Küstenfliegergruppen*, the momentum that the German propaganda had generated in the meantime overshadowed any future reference by the press to them and their part in the operation.

Throughout the period, various elements of the *Gruppe* were transferred for a multitude of operational requirements. On 1 October 1939, 2./306 was transferred to Wittensee, where it took on the responsibilities of 2./406, which had been based there up until that time.

The *Gruppe*'s Only Loss

On 22 September, 1./306 was detailed to perform a reconnaissance of the Danzig Bay area. For the operation, the *Staffel* had assigned *Oblt* Gerhard Grosse and *Lt.z.S* Helmut von Rabenau to fly He 60 K6+QH (WNr 6247) as part of the first wave of reconnaissance in the area. Operating to the east of the *Staffel* was to be aircraft of 1./506, which had been detailed to concentrate on the Hela peninsula. Takeoff was scheduled for early afternoon. However, Grosse soon ran into difficulties with the engine of the He 60. Unable to make friendly landfall, he had no choice but to force land off Kaaseberga, near the Swedish town of Kivik. Gross and von Rabenau were both rescued by the Swedes, but were interned and not repatriated to Germany until 8 July 1940. K6+QH meanwhile was taken under tow by the Swedish torpedo boat *Vidar*. It was taken to Ystad and moored until 4 November 1940, whereupon it was returned to Germany. This incident represented the only wartime loss suffered by the *Gruppe*.

Obsolete

On 22 October, as part of the reorganisation of the German naval air forces, the three units of *Küstenfliegergruppe* 306 ceased to exist. At the end of October, the *Stab./306* became *Stab./406*, while 1./306 became 3./806. For 2./306, there would be no reincarnation under another guise. Orders were received that the personnel, aircraft, and equipment of the unit were to be transferred to other units as and where the need arose.

While the combat life of the *Gruppe* was short-lived, it had committed itself well and suffered just one loss. Although marginalised by the activities of other *Staffeln*, it nonetheless earned respect as an efficient and well organised unit that had played a vital role in the campaign against Poland in September and October 1939, as well as an over-looked but impressive reconnaissance role in the west.

7

Küstenfliegergruppe 406

One of the oldest *Küstenfliegergruppen*, the 1 *Staffel* of the unit, was created on 1 April 1937. Three months later, this was followed in July with the creation of the *Stab* and two further *Staffeln*. Like all pre-war units, the *Gruppe* was equipped as any other with He 60, Do 18, and He 59 aircraft for the 1, 2, and 3 *Staffeln* respectively. Similarly, the crews of each unit maintained a regular programme of flying, attending lectures, and exercise so as to remain proficient in all areas. By the outbreak of war, the various *Staffeln* were all stationed at List, and it was the 1 *Staffel* that held the honour within the *Gruppe* of being first on operations during the morning of 1 September 1939.

War

At 04:35 hours on the morning of the invasion of Poland, 1./406 launched aircraft X, W,V, U, T, S, R, and Q on a reconnaissance sortie. Instructions relayed to the crews now meant that any vessel encountered was subject to a variety of procedures. Whereas pre-war practice had seen aircrew log all details of any vessels observed during a sortie on their maps, observers were instructed to note only neutral shipping in such a manner. Meanwhile, all friendly vessels were to be noted verbally upon return of the crew, and any positively identified Polish vessels were to be considered hostile. While close attention was paid to a multitude of variable situations, the first operation of the war by the *Gruppe* returned having sighted only Scandinavian ships, with no sign of either convoys sailing to Poland or Polish ships attempting to flee. Thus, the *Gruppe* fell into a routine as *F.d.L West* maintained a vigilant watch against any British operations in

Mechanics service a pre-war He 60. On the nose is the early style crest employed by
1./406. (*Via D. Wadman*)

Crew prepare a Dornier 18 for a pre-war flight. Evident on the engine cowling is the
early version of the 2./506 emblem.

the North Sea, while the majority of German strength was concentrated against Poland. However, on 26 September the crew of He 60 K6+XH became embroiled in a tragic accident.

Returning from patrol, the crew observed a twin-engine, dark coloured aircraft. The unidentified observer later recorded in the war diary:

> While flying back to base I saw in grid 9333 a twin-engine, low-wing aircraft on course of 240° (single tail plane). It pulled up into cloud at 700 m, but [we] followed. The aircraft was seen again 300m higher and with course correction of 30°. [We] continued to follow and attempted to identify the aircraft. The opponent was flying faster (approx. 300 kph). No identification markings could be seen. At a distance of 300 m [we] opened fire, but there was no reaction from the opponent. Then both aircraft became separated in the clouds. [We] kept up the chase flying on a course of 300°. The opponent was sighted again 300 m on the starboard side. [We] opened fire again from astern and below. The opponent throttled back and simultaneously [we] saw the letters 'PH'. [We] ceased fire and turned towards base.

Unbeknownst to the crew, the aircraft they had attacked was the Dutch DC-3 flight PH-ASM. When the DC-3 landed at Amsterdam, a total of about thirty machine-gun hits were found, including hits in the oil and fuel tanks. Tragically, the Swedish citizen Gustav Robert Lamm, aged thirty-eight, had been killed during the combat.

While such incidents were rare, they highlighted the difficulties faced by crews. Other difficulties remained the weather. With the need to transfer reconnaissance data and photographs to higher command and intelligence centres in Wilhelmshaven, crews relied on second-line aircraft, such as the W34 and Ju 52. However, standing orders within the *Gruppe* were such that all flights in these types of aircraft engaged on the transfer of documents had to be completed at least 1-hour prior to sundown. If the weather turned foul it meant crews and pilots could be stranded from their home base for several days. However, the more important difficulty faced was the inter-service rivalry between the *Luftwaffe* and *Kriegsmarine* for control of the naval air arm, and it was no better illustrated than on 21 October 1939.

During the daily reconnaissance, *Luftwaffe* aircraft had found a convoy steaming north off Flamborough Head. As ships sailing in convoy could be attacked without warning, the naval staff sought permission to intercept the ships. Permission was granted but it was decided to develop the raid and make it a joint attack by He 115s and Ju 88s equipped with conventional bombs. As the Ju 88s had a higher cruising speed than the lumbering seaplanes, the plan called for a staggered start, thereby allowing

The flight line of 3./406 He 59s. The early style emblem used by the unit was the same as that used by 3./506.

the Heinkels to intercept the convoy shortly by the Junkers. However, as with all things planned in moderation, the plan fell apart when put in an extreme situation. At 12:35 hours, three Ju 88s of I./KG 30 were launched, each with a bomb load of two SC500 bombs. Shortly before their takeoff, 1./406 launched nine He 115s, each equipped with two SC250 bombs. Unfortunately for the crews, the Junkers appeared over the convoy first, thereby alerting the British defences. These included the Spitfires of A-Flight of No. 72 Squadron, based at Leconfield, and Hurricanes of No. 46 Squadron based at North Coates who were on patrol nearby. While the three Ju 88s managed to escape before the Spitfires could intervene in a meaningful sense, the lumbering Heinkels flew into heavy defensive actions by the British. In the ensuing dogfight, the following four He 115s were lost: S4+EH (WNr. 1882), whose crew, *Lt* Fritz Meyer (F), *Oblt.z.S* Heinz Schlicht (B), and *Uffz* Bernhard Wessels (Bf), were all killed; S4+GH (WNr. 2093) was forced down on the sea and *Fw* Rolf Findeisen (F) was captured badly injured, *Oblt.z.S* Günther Remann (B) captured slightly injured, and *Uffz* Hans Schultze (Bf) captured unhurt; S4+DH (WNr. 1887) crashed during an attempted ditching, with *Uffz* Günther Pahnke (F) and *Oblt.z.S* Albert Peinemann (B) both captured slightly injured and *Uffz* Hermann Einhaus (Bf) captured unhurt; S4+YH (WNr. 1876) ditched near the Danish vessel *Dagmar Clausen*. While *Uffz* Peter Grossgarts (F) and *Lt.z.S* Gottfried Lenz (B) were both rescued (the latter slightly injured) and returned to Germany two days later, no trace was found of *Uffz* Helmut Becker (Bf).

The loss of so many aircrew was a hammer-blow for the *Staffel* and served to further emphasise the underperformance of naval aircraft types. While the nine He 115s had been attacked by a dozen fighters and the losses could have been a lot worse, a more worrying sign was the susceptibility of German maritime aircraft against a variety of British types. On 10 November, Do 18 K6+DL (WNr. 0804) of 3./406 was lost when it was intercepted east-north-east of Scarborough by a Lockheed Hudson aircraft of No. 220 Squadron. As the pilot *Fw* Jakob Pelzer later recorded:

I flew as a tactical Nr. 2 as ordered. At 10:30 hours we reached the first waypoint at an altitude of 50 m. At 11:15 hours, two English scouts (type Lockheed 14) were sighted ahead. The airplanes attacked from behind and above and dead ahead owing to their superior speed. I made

The personnel of 2./406 assemble for the funeral of a fallen comrade. Unfortunately, services such as this were a common occurrence. Date unknown.

combat turns that were very slow, however, because our fuel level was only now 2,000 litres. In a head-on pass, four hits were clearly observed. Out of the front and rear of the aircraft a fire started. The rear M. G. became inoperable after the first drum was fired. The fire from the English airplane was opened beyond a range of 500 m. The attack was broken off at a distance of about 200-300 m. In the first attack, our Dornier received some hits mid-ship. In the navigation room, the impact was light. The auxiliary observer tried to radio a distress, but was unable. At the same time, the rear motor lost power and shut down. I could not maintain height and so had to make an emergency landing. During the landing, the stern touched down first, but we bounced and landed again on the bow. I do not know what happened to the observer, but I think he fell out when we hit the water. I saw him floating there and his face was bloody. We all got out of the aircraft and got in the rubber dinghy, however I could no longer see the observer. The water was now above the water-rudder and at the nose of the aircraft. It started to list to starboard and after 45 minutes it sank. After the attack, a British aircraft remained in the area for about 2 hours; the other flew to England immediately after the engagement. We saw another aircraft (letter C – Staffel unknown) and fired red flares, but they were not seen. We also saw another Do 18, but again failed to attract its attention. In the evening, we saw the steamer *Jeanette*. We shot red and green flares, which were seen. The steamer found us and took us aboard. The reception was sincere and we got hot water, warm clothing, and food. On the Saturday, we were interned in Vlieland. We were treated good there as well.

The crew of *Uffz* Walter Kliesch (Bf), *Fw* Christian Kleff (Bm), and Pelzer were eventually returned to Germany, although no trace was found of the observer *Oblt.z.S* Wilhelm Lütjens.

The losses continued to mount throughout 1939 as it became increasingly clear that operations in daylight hours close to the English coastline were unsustainable. On 13 November, *Uffz* Homes was wounded by machine gun bullets from a No. 56 Squadron Hurricane of Harwich when his Do 18 K6+AK (WNr. 0838) was intercepted. Later inspection revealed some sixty hits to the airframe. In December, the *Gruppe* sustained three further incidents with a ditching in the North Sea due to engine failure and two further aircraft intercepted and damaged by Hurricanes. However, as the winter closed in flying conditions deteriorated and the pace of operations slowed. At this time, administratively *Stab./406* was given the responsibility of overseeing the development of the long-range *Transozean Staffel*. The unit had been raised with the intention of supplying reconnaissance and transport duties with the Dornier 26 flying boat and Ha 139 seaplane.

The Blohm and Voss Ha 139 'Nordwind' was part of the *Trans Ozean Staffel* which came under the command of Stab./406 in 1940.

With so few of these types available, the development process was slow and tedious. By early January 1940, these aircraft were still not operational and it would be some time before they joined operations.

The new year brought little change, and as the winter months gave way to spring, the *Gruppe* worked towards improving its serviceability. At the same time, the Germans began preparing for the invasion of Scandinavia. To this end, operational reconnaissance sorties focused on the Royal Navy and its activities in the North Sea. This was particularly important in early April 1940, as the German ships employed in the invasion of Norway had sailed a few days before. On 7 April, the *Gruppe* launched eighteen sorties to the Peterhead-Shetland area to ascertain whether the launching of so many German ships had earned a response from the British. The only response appeared to be when Do 18 K6+JK was significantly damaged by Hudsons of No. 220 Squadron over the North Sea in the mid-afternoon. Two days later, on the opening day of the invasion, 9 April, the *Gruppe* could only manage ten sorties, the first of which launched from Hörnum at 05:20 hours. These were designed to protect the German landings along the Norwegian coastline and scout for enemy activity. Unfortunately, Do 18 K6+HL was shot down by gunners aboard a No. 9 Squadron Wellington returning from a raid; *Oblt* Heinrich de Vlieger (F), *Lt.z.S* Wolfgang Ochrs

(B), *Uffz* Hanz Liesner (h.B), and *Fw* Helmut Suhr (Bm) all perished. The loss of crew in what could only have been the clumsiest of dogfights imaginable only served to emphasise the pitiful state of the aircraft crews were forced to fly. This loss was followed up on 17 April when Do 18 K6+FH (WNr. 836) of 1./406 was lost after it was intercepted by Skuas from No. 801 Squadron, Fleet Air Arm. Suffering from engine damage, the pilot *Fw* Karl Petersen attempted to make an emergency landing on the sea, however crashed in doing so. Petersen, along with *Lt.z.S* Max Keil (B), *Fk.Ogfr* Werner Merg (h.B), and *Uffz* Jacob Ims (Bm), was killed.

Throughout the summer months, the *Gruppe* continued as it had before. The difficulty it faced remained the obsolete Do 18 flying boat. During May, the *Transozean Staffel* was turned over to the administrative control of *Kampfgruppe zur besonderen Verwendung 6*. Increasingly though, operations were moved further offshore of the British coastline in an effort to offer a modicum of protection to the Dornier. To a certain degree this worked, with only one loss incurred by the *Gruppe* during the whole of May, none in June, and only one in July. However, there was no accounting for the fact the Dorniers were obsolete and in desperate need of replacement.

At the end of May, with operations in Norway moving decidedly in favour of the Germans, 2./406 was transferred from Hörnum to Stavanger. This move coincided with an identical move by 3./406. The Germans intended to use the obvious advantages of Norwegian seaplane harbours to further the range of aerial reconnaissance into the northern Atlantic

A flight of Dornier 18 aircraft of 2./406 on patrol in spring 1940.

Above and below: Aircraft of 2./406 form up for a wartime operation.

in support of U-boat operations there. Meanwhile, Rantum remained the main base of operations for 1./406.

With the onset of the Battle of Britain, it became obvious more support was needed for air-sea rescue services. As a result, by August elements of the *Gruppe* were occasionally detailed for search and rescue operations. To better supply this sort of support, in early September 1940 3./406 was transferred to the Dutch base at Schellingwoude/Amsterdam to support *Luftflotte* 2. This humanitarian element did not preclude them from misfortune. On 5 September, Do 18 K6+KL (WNr 0874) of 3./406 was attacked by four Blenheim aircraft off Calais during the early evening. *Uffz* Heinrich Thiermann (F) and *Oblt.z.S.* Max Dietrich (B) were both wounded in the melee, although the Dornier did not sustain serious damage, being declared operational again on 18 September.

The difficulties associated with Dornier operations were soon recognised, and on 29 September 3./406 received orders that it was to re-equip with the Heinkel He 115 seaplane. It was hoped that such a process would better support the German's war against trade. However, the planned conversion did not materialise and the *Staffel* was forced to retain its flying boats. This presented the Germans with a major setback, as the He 115, however unsuitable, was the only aircraft available for torpedo operations in either the North Sea or Atlantic approaches. This was especially frustrating for *Stab./406*, as by the end of the year it had under its command 1./106, 2./506, and 1./906, all of which were He 115-equipped *Staffeln*. However, none of the successes these units scored did much to further the reputation of *Küstenfliegergruppe* 406. By the close of 1940, the *Kommandeur* of the *Gruppe Oberstleutnant* Karl Stockmann was complaining so bitterly about the effectiveness of seaplanes that he requested one of his *Staffel* convert to the long-range, land-based Fw 200. With that aircraft type in short supply, the request was denied.

1941: New Operational Regions, New Aircraft

The first two months of 1941 saw the transfer from Norway of 1./406 to List and 2./406 to Hörnum. In both instances, this signalled a change in fortunes, with both units converting from the Do 18 to the He 115 (1./406) and Bv 138 (2./406). In both instances, the transfer took about three months. Once completed, 1./406 moved to Søreisa, about halfway between Tromsø and Narvik, while 2./406 moved to Trondheim. Once returned to Norway, the units began to undertake more regular and meaningful operations over the Arctic and North Atlantic. Meanwhile, 3./406 continued to struggle with the Do 18 flying boat, and it would not be until the close of the year it would return to Germany to re-equip with the Bv 138. On 17 February, the unit had been moved from Schellingwoude to Trondheim to partially offset the loss of the other two *Staffeln* as they undertook their conversion process. The run of incidents associated with the out-dated Dorniers continued to hamper the *Gruppe*. On 31 March 1941, the aft-engine of WNr 0858 failed, causing it to crash in a failed attempt to ditch. *Ogfr* Max Reisner (Bf) was killed, while *Ofw* Christian Klaff (Bm) was injured. Although without the loss of life associated, the same fate befell a 2./406 machine (WNr 0861) as it was on patrol over the Skagerrak on 2 April. However, these proved the only two mechanical-related losses of the year for the type. The only other non-combat incident occurred on 14 May when WNr 0896 of 3./406 was forced to make an emergency landing on Trondheim Fjord due to inclement weather. While there were no injuries, the aircraft was slightly damaged.

In June 1941, opportunities arose for further anti-shipping operations in the Baltic with the invasion of Soviet Russia. This operation had severely drained the resources in the west and placed increase pressure on air units in the east. While on 28 June, the strength of 1./406 stood at nine He 115s, only four were serviceable for use by the three crews operational. This level of proficiency was undermined when on 8 August it became necessary to temporarily transfer three aircraft and crews to

A Do 18 of 2./506 loaded aboard a catapult vessel and ready for another operation. Catapult vessels allowed aircraft to be launched in a shorter space and when weather conditions precluded normal take off procedures from water.

the *Luftwaffe*'s *Aufklärungsgruppe* 125, based in Riga. This transfer was designed to better facilitate offensive operations against Soviet shipping in the Baltic. Similar operational requirements later led to the transfer of 1, 3./506, and 2./906 for the same purposes during September. Over the next few weeks, the three crews were in constant action. In total, they flew twenty-two missions, used twelve torpedoes, two of which found their mark, suffered five torpedo failures, and similarly missed five times.

At the same time, in the west the RAF's Coastal Command began to develop a presence in the region, and more and more frequently the *Seeflieger* chanced upon Allied aircraft. While often combat proved inconclusive, the threat they posed was not ignored. The day after the three crews were transferred to Riga, Do 18 K6+AL (WNr 0869) of 3./406 was lost without a trace on a sortie to the east coast of Britain. On board was *Uffz* Herbert Guhl (F), *Lt* Peter von Nottbeck, *Ogfr* Georg Glück (bf), and *Uffz* Hubert Glöser (Bm). The cause of the loss is not known.

1942

By the end of the year, the three *Staffeln* had all be re-equipped and were now based in Norway. Meanwhile, the *Stabsstaffeln* was in Brest-Süd, but not in control of its own *Staffeln*. For the operational units, the order of the day remained anti-shipping and reconnaissance operations, although in the mountainous regions of Norway, the weather over the winter often precluded operations. A report by 1./406 for 8 January noted the weather had previously been unfavourable for operations, yet it was to be assumed that the following readiness orders would be adhered to irrespective: 1. Night reconnaissance of four airplanes with six pilots on standby; 2. 3-hour readiness for blind-flying with three airplanes; 3. A single airplane on 4-hour readiness for reconnaissance; 4. Stand by aircraft to be maintained. All this by a *Staffel* that had thirteen aircraft and crews available on the day. Such high serviceability rates reflected the inactivity of the unit, as mostly the aircraft and crews suffered from conditions and a lack of supplies. As the weather improved, the situation changed as operations could recommence. By March, only two He 115s of eight were serviceable for operations by 1./406, while 2./406 could only boast two Bv 138s of ten serviceable. The need for reliable aircraft was of paramount importance, as the crews increasingly found themselves on the hunt for Allied convoys headed to Russia. During the winter months, the polar ice cap forced the convoys to sail closer to German bases in Norway, yet during the summer months, a much more northerly course could be set. By May 1942, between the three *Staffeln*, sixteen aircraft were available from operations from a total of twenty-one. This type of operational readiness provided a reasonable platform for anti-convoy work. However, the limited reconnaissance availability in the region was a point of much tension between the *Luftwaffe* and *Kriegsmarine*. As late as 10 June 1942, the *Luftwaffe* had advised German command in Norway that, 'Additional reconnaissance forces cannot be furnished, and under no circumstances are bombers to be used for reconnaissance tasks only.' This attitude only served to heighten the difficulties faced in the region and coordination between air and sea forces operating against Allied shipping. However, success was close at hand.

Convoy PQ 17 had sailed from Hvalfjord in Iceland on 27 June, and consisted of thirty-five vessels. Since early on the morning of 2 July, the *Staffelkapitän* of 1./406, *Hptm* Herbert Vater, and two other aircraft had been in contact with the convoy and were shadowing its movements. In Norway, offensive operations were planned, which included a sortie by the German battleship *Tirpitz* and supporting fleet units, as well as air operations. Included in this battle plan was torpedo operations by the He 115s of 1./406. The attack was launched in the afternoon and a total of eight sorties were flown by the *Staffel* against PQ 17. However, He 115 (WNr 2759) was shot down not far from the convoy. In a daring feat of airmanship and camaraderie, the crew, who had taken to their dinghy, was rescued when *Fw* Konrad Arabin landed his He 115 close by, and under the noses of the watching Allies, rescued the hapless crew. It was in no small part due to the reconnaissance and torpedo operations of 1./406 that resounding success was achieved against PQ 17, with twenty-four of its number sunk by combined air and U-boat operations.

Combined operations between the *Küstenflieger* and *Kriegsmarine* sometimes produced unusual results. The normal plan was that aircraft would furnish reconnaissance data for use by U-boats in formulating their attacks. However, on 16 August one crew of 3./406 found themselves in need of help from the U-boats. Ordered to determine the limits of floating ice in the Arctic and to scout for enemy shipping, Bv 138 7R+CH (WNr 310024) had landed to refuel from U-255 in position 73° N, 00° E. Yet after the procedure had been completed, it was found that technical problems precluded the aircraft from taking off. In discussion with the U-boat's captain *Kptnlt* Reinhart Reche it was decided to tow the aircraft back to friendly waters, where it could be taken to a repair facility. The Bv 138 was consequently taken under tow, but the aircraft sank in difficult seas. It wasn't until 9 September that the aircrew landed ashore when U-255 entered Neidenfjord in southern Norway. Such fortuitous luck could not always be counted upon. On 4 November, Bv 138 K6+GK (WNr 130132) of 3./406 disappeared during a routine patrol to the east of Iceland. Its

A mid-Atlantic meeting between a Bv 138 and two U-boats. Scenes such as this were uncommon, although occasionally aircrew rendezvoused with U-boats to refuel the diesel-powered aircraft. Operations such as this allowed increase range. This particular aircraft is 6I+KK (Wnr 311039) belonging to 2./SAGr 130, the rebranded 2./706. The two U-boats are U-255 and U-601. On 16 August 1942, U-255 participated in the rescue of the crew of 7R+CH, which had force-landed due to mechanical troubles. (*Via D. Wadman*)

crew of *Uffz* Werner Scholz (F), *Lt* Friedrich Lohmeyer (B), *Uffz* Paul Kron (Bf), *Ofw* Wilhelm Hofmann (Bm), and *Uffz* Rudolf Wendler (Bm) were all listed as missing. From this date until the end of the year, the *Gruppe* lost a total of six aircraft to various means (three to storm damage over Christmas), but fortunately no human life was lost.

1943

In October 1942, the *Stabsstaffel* had been disbanded, though appeared to be no imminent threat to the combat *Staffeln*. Still based in Norway, the units continued operations as and when the winter weather allowed. On 24 January, the He 115s were again in action against a convoy, this time JW

52, which had left Liverpool on 17 January. Attacking in limited strength, K6+EH (WNr 1864) and K6+MH (WNr 2733) were both shot down by the defences. *Ofw* Kurt Riedel (F), *Lt* Hans-Georg Schmidt (B), *Uffz* Hans-Joachim Gottlieb (Bf), *Ofw* Hans Broy (F), *Lt* Arno Kratz (B), and *Uffz* Kurt Kleismann (Bf) all perished in the icy waters before help could arrive. These losses presaged a growing number of losses that the various *Staffeln* were to suffer throughout 1943. Predominantly, these would be borne by 2 and 3./406 with their long-range Bv 138 flying boats. Consequently, neither unit could muster more than nine aircraft in any given month in the first half of 1943.While a steady stream of replacements was on hand, at times they were not with their respective *Staffeln* very long. On 3 April, Bv 138 (WNr 311017) was lost along with the crew of *Lt* Gerhard Feist (F), *Uffz* Walter Wirt (B), *Ofw* Willi Eck (Bf), *Ofw* Georg Kircher (Bm), and *Uffz* Albert Bode (Bm). The aircraft was still wearing its factory codes of NA+PO and had not had its unit codes applied. These losses reflected the growing capabilities of the Allies, both in terms of defensive fire from escorts and merchant ships and patrols by British and American aircraft.

A Harrowing Few Weeks

The increased naval presence in the Atlantic meant reconnaissance flights had to be careful not just of land-based patrols, but also the possibility of fighters launched from aircraft carriers. On 28 July, three Bv 138s of 2./706 had set out to search for a British Task Force that had been reported near the Shetlands. One of these was K6+BK (WNr 0311047), which had been catapult-launched from 'Bussard' armed with six SC50 bombs. Takeoff was for mid-morning, but as the aircraft approach the Shetlands from the north-north-east, it was intercepted by Flt Off. Keefe in his No. 404 Squadron Beaufighter in position 63°03´00 N, 02°37´30 E. With his aircraft crippled, the German pilot *Fw* Klaus Kopatzki was able to force land on the sea, allowing the crew to take to their dinghy. As the plane went down, a distress signal was sent. Fortuitously, cruising nearby was the Type XIV U-boat U-489, commanded by *Lt* Adalbert Schmandt. Having picked up the distress signal, Schmandt moved to rescue the downed crew and *Lt.z.S* Hans Knittell (B), *Uffz* Heinz Hengst (Bf), and *Uffz* Werner Mohlau (Bs) were saved. Unfortunately, Kopatzki and the flight mechanic *Ofw* Werner Hennrich were killed when the centre engine, damaged in the attack, broke free from its mountings and collapsed into the cockpit on touch-down. Far from being safe, the three crew members now faced a long patrol aboard the U-boat, and it was not long before they were to taste the ferocity of the Battle of the Atlantic. On 3 August at 07:50 hours, the U-boat was attacked while on the surface south-east of Iceland by a British Catalina of No. 190 Squadron. The British crew reported hits in a strafing run on the boat, but sustained damage to their aircraft from the defensive AA put up by the Germans, forcing their withdrawal. As the Catalina flew off, a Hudson of No. 269 Squadron engaged the boat with bombs and gunfire. This badly damaged the U-boat, which was forced to dive. Just over 24 hours later, the U-boat again came under attack, this time by a Canadian Sunderland of No. 423 Squadron. Again the Germans manned their AA guns, and while they succeeded in shooting down the aircraft, the U-boat was badly damaged. In view of the damage, and with the British destroyers HMS *Castleton* and *Orwell* closing in, Schmandt had no choice but to order the boat be abandoned. In the end, all but one of those aboard the boat were rescued and made prisoners; the boats chief engineer *Oblt* Mude was mortally injured setting off scuttling charges and died soon after.

The task force the Germans had set out to find was Force A, which consisted of two battleships (HMS *Anson* and USS *Alabama*), the carrier HMS *Illustrious*, and eight destroyers (USS *Rodman*, USS *Macomb*, USS *Emmons*, USS *Fitch*, HMS *Milne*, HMS *Musketeer*, HMS *Meteor,* and HMS *Mahratta*). The Allied plan had been to simulate a raid on Norway, thereby luring out the German battleship *Tirpitz*. Although the Germans did not take the bait, they made repeated efforts to maintain contact with Force A. In doing so, five aircraft were shot down – all of them from 2./406. These included K6+BK (WNr 311047), K6+CK (WNr 310109), K6+GK

Silhouetted by the early evening skyline, a Bv 138 of 3./406 returns from patrol.

(WNr 311027) K6+KK, (WNr 310090), and K6+HH (WNr 311026). The loss of twenty-five aircrew and five aircraft was a significant blow for the *Staffel*, and for the brief period following the loss operations by 2./406 were severely restricted. In fact, so desperate was the plight of the *Staffel* that orders had been issued to redesignate 2 and 3./406 as *Luftwaffe* units. The former became 3./*Seeaufklärungsgruppe* 130, while the latter became the 1./*Seeaufklärungsgruppe* 131. This left the He 115-equipped 1./406 as the last surviving *Küstenfliegerstaffel*; all others had been appropriated or absorbed into the *Luftwaffe*.

Sole Survivor

With the transfer to *Luftwaffe* control, the members of 1./406 knew time would soon be up for them too. However, this did not affect their performance or dedication to duty. At the same time, the unit was moved from Kirkenes to Hommelvik. Despite the growing odds stacked against them, the crews of the unit continued to maintain a reconnaissance presence in the Atlantic and Arctic Oceans. *Staffelkapitän Hptm* Christian Fischer flew regularly, but was lost on 4 October 1943 when K6+MH (WNr 1866) was shot down by American naval pilots from an altitude of 200 m. While the loss of life was deplorable, the conversion to other types by some units and the disbandment of others meant there was a greater supply of parts for the unit. Thus by the end of the month, the unit had on strength twelve aircraft, of which nine were serviceable.

As 1943 gave way to 1944, an increasing part of the *Staffel*'s role was escort duties for German naval forces along the Norwegian coastline. Increasingly, Allied intelligence began receiving reports of aircraft shepherding merchant shipping and U-boats in and about Norwegian waters. Such operations lasted for hours and were often conducted in pairs so that at no stage were naval forces left unattended.

Throughout 1944, the unit continued to operate to the best of its abilities, but with the invasion of Continental Europe in June, it became increasingly clear that the Germans were fighting a lost cause. Much of the material needed to conduct an effective war in the Atlantic was being channeled to other fronts. As a result, by October 1944 man-power for the land war in Europe and the east was forcing the Germans to cast a wider net for recruits. In that month, as part of a reorganisation of manpower the final *Küstenfliegerstaffel*, 1./406, was disbanded and its members were dispersed to other units.

8

Küstenfliegergruppe 506

During the rapid expansion of the *Luftwaffe* in the 1930s, several new *Küstenfliegerstaffeln* were created. Rather than completely new identities, many were old maritime units in a new guise. Originally formed in Dievenow from the *Stab* and 1 *Staffel* of *Küstenfliegergruppe* 306, the first two *Staffeln* of *Küstenfliegergruppe* 506 reflected this practice. While the *Stab./*506 was a non-flying unit, the 1./506 was equipped with He 60s. Completing the new *Gruppe*, in December of that year the 2 and 3 *Staffeln* were raised. However, these units were raised from scratch. Based at Kamp and Pillau respectively, the two new *Staffeln* were in the tradition of *Küstenfliegergruppen* doctrine. While the 2./506 was equipped with the Do 18 for long-range reconnaissance, the 3./506 was equipped with the general purpose He 59.

As the political situation in Europe deteriorated in the late 1930s, crews of the unit began intensifying their training. Not merely focused on flying, each *Staffelkapitane* prepared regular lectures for his airmen. The topics ranged from political discussions to mechanical engineering. In addition, crews undertook regular revision of aircraft identification. Despite this, during the early months of the war crews regularly misidentified British aircraft they had encountered while on patrol. However to offset this, each *Staffeln* had at least one member who had seen service during the Spanish Civil War. The most prominent of these were Günther 'Savvy' Krech and Karl-Heinrich Schneider, both of whom served in the opening phases of the war with 3./506. The *Ritterkreuzträger* Schneider was lost with all fifty crew members of U-522 when it was sunk in the mid-Atlantic, south-west of Madeira, Portugal, 31°27′ N 26°22′ W, by depth charges from the British sloop HMS *Totland* on 23 February 1943 with the rank of *Kapitänleutnant*. Yet the similarly-ranked Krech survived the war after

Ground crew work on preparing a pre-war He 60 of 1./506 for another sortie. Clearly visible on the engine cowling is the emblem for the *Staffel* – a red winged griffon on a white shield.

Hauptman Hermann Busch, *Staffelkapitän* of 1./506 during September 1939. Bush transferred as the *Staffelkapitän* of 1./806 on New Year's Day 1940.

he was rescued by Canadian destroyer HMCS *Athabascan* and taken prisoner with four survivors of the U- 558, which was sunk in the Bay of Biscay, north-west of Cape Ortegal, Spain, 45°10′ N 09°24′ W, by depth charges from a British Halifax from 58 Squadron RAF and a US Liberator aircraft from 19 A/S Squadron USAF on 20 July 1943.

By August 1939, the unit was flying regular patrols over the Baltic. Increasingly, the unit was tasked with identifying shipping in the region. To do this, on the eve of the Polish Campaign 1./506, which was under the command of *Hptm* Hermann Busch, had on strength twelve He 60s, of which ten were serviceable. *Hptm* Herbert Hartwig's 2./506 had eleven serviceable Do 18s from a total of twelve, while *Hptm* Ludwig Fehling had nine serviceable He 59s available for operations by 3./506 from a total of ten.

The Polish Campaign

To provide naval air support for *Fall Weiß*, the *Luftwaffe* assigned *Generalmajor* Coeler (*Führer der Luft Ost*) fifty floatplanes. Included within this total was *Küstenfliegergruppe* 506, minus the 2 *Staffeln*, which was subordinate to *Stab./706*, itself assigned to *Führer der Luft West*. Alerted the previous evening, in the early hours of 1 September 1939 1./506 was at readiness with ten aircraft, while all nine serviceable aircraft of the 3./506 were at readiness. Although the latter did not fly operationally during the day, by 05:00 hours 1./506 had launched reconnaissance sorties towards the Danzig Bight searching for Polish shipping and to reconnoiter enemy coastal positions. It did not take long for the unit to experience its first enemy contact. At 06:09 hours, He 60 M7+RH of 1./506 was fired upon after encountering two destroyers, two submarines, and five mine sweepers in the Danzig Bight. While no damage was sustained and the aircraft returned safely, this represented only a minor part in operations conducted that day. In total, 1./506 amassed 45 hours and 25 minutes of combat air time from a total of fifteen sorties throughout the day.

The predominant focus during the opening days of the campaign was in reducing the garrison at Gdingen and naval batteries at Hela. Following the rigors of the opening day, on 2 September 1./506 was again alerted for operations similar in design to the opening day of combat. Operations for the day had been scheduled for takeoff at 08:30 hours by three sections of aircraft. While the other elements lifted off without incident, at 08:36 hours pilot *Uffz* Ernst August Damrau and his observer *Lt.d.R* Hoffman were killed when their He 60, M7+NH (WNr. 1463), crashed on takeoff. The report submitted by the *Staffelkapitän* to *ObdM* stated:

Aircraft He 60 D: engine BMW 6 M 18 435. Crew: *Lt.d.Res.* Hoffmann

Aircrew of 1./506 stand in front of a He 60 from the unit. Members include *Ofw* Siegwarth, *Oblt* Stricker, *Oblt* Laver, *Lt* Magnussen, *Lt.z.S* Bärner, *Uffz* Monning, *Ofw* Kröning, Hasenberg, *Ofw* Bonezyk, *Hptm* Busch, *Ofw* Batterbradt, *Lt.z.S* Queer-Fastern, *Uffz* Grabbe, Mammen, *Lt.z.S* Pich, *Lt* Hattenbach, *Oblt* Tantzen, *Uffz* Kunze.

(B), *Uffz.* Damrau (F) – aircraft crashed against harbour pier in Pillau-Neutief on takeoff at 0830 hrs for a reconnaissance sortie over Danzig Bight. Plane was damaged by fire. The crew perished. Possible reason: the plane probably swung off and lifted off too late hitting the pier with floats. Weather situation: clear…

This first loss hit the *Staffel* hard. In only the second day of war, the unit was faced with the realities of combat. Despite the loss, throughout the day 1 *Staffel* flew nine sorties, totaling 32 hours and 19 minutes. Meanwhile, 3./506 was finally involving itself in combat flying ten sorties, totaling 18 hours and 32 minutes. Its report of operations for the day was as concise as they were insightful:

Short combat report about night bomb attack by 3./506 on Gdingen on 2.9.39: 1st section started individual attacks at 0215 hrs from altitudes of 1800-2800 m, attack course: E or SW. An explosion in old military harbour as well as on the ground was observed. Navy HQ was probably hit. No defences. 2nd section made individual attacks between 03:14 and 03:21 hours. Attack altitudes: 2800-3200 m. Attack course: SE. Explosions in old military harbour and in new military harbour were observed. Five to six searchlights were on for 15 seconds after the attack carried out by leading plane. 3rd section attacked between 0335 and 0350 hrs. Attack altitudes: 1200-3000 m. Attack course: NE, S, and SE. Hits within the area of the new and old military harbor. Part of the bombs that had been dropped by the last plane did not detonate, presumably due to failure of Z.S.K. (1200 m). Four searchlights and four flak batteries engaged the aircraft.

Visibility was good during approach, but during the attack insufficient. According to information from the military intelligence centre at Königsberg, explosions were observed in old military harbor at 03;10 hours and 03:15 hours in the direction of Oxhöf.

From before the war, the Germans acknowledged the need to reduce the Polish naval and land forces in and around Hel. For the Germans, the main consternation remained the presence of naval forces in the harbour of Hel. On 1 September, the Polish mine-layer ORP *Gryf,* the destroyer ORP *Wicher,* two gunboats (the *Komendant Pilsudski* and *General Haller),* and six minesweepers (*Czajka, Rybitwa, Mewa, Czapla, Jaskolka,* and *Zuraw*) were attacked by Ju 87 dive bombers from *Lehrgerschwader* 1. During the attack, ORP *Gryf,* which was loaded with 290 mines, was damaged by near misses. With its rudder jammed, machinery telegraph, compasses, and radio station damaged, *Gryf* entered Hel harbour for repairs. With raids by 3./706 and 4./186 targeting the ships over the next 48 hours, the German destroyers *Leberecht Maaß* and *Wolfgang Zenker* were sent to intercept the Polish forces. However, after a brief battle in which the German destroyers were engaged by both shore batteries and the *Wicher,* both ships were forced to withdraw with damage. As a result, a further raid against these ships was ordered. At 09:10 hours, 11 Ju 87s, escorted by four Bf 109T from II./186, attacked, and *Gryf* sustained one bomb hit on the bow and several near-misses, which set her on fire. The fire reached the AAA ammunition, which detonated, but dock and ship remained afloat. Frustrated by the lack of success, the Germans sent in another raid by ten Ju 87s of 4./186, which finally succeeded in sinking the destroyer *Wicher.* Then at 16:00 hours, 3./506 sent in nine aircraft in three flights of three to bomb the harbour installations and the *Gryf.* The unit later reported that, 'High-level attack (nine aircraft) in vics [sic] line astern from an altitude of approx. 3000 m, course: west. Two hits

A flight of three pre-war He 60s on an operation over a dense layer of cloud. The height at which these aircraft are operating suggests this was a training exercise not connected with reconnaissance duties.

in outer mole, two hits in promenade. Two hits between *Gryf* and pier.' This further damage was added to by 3./706, which attacked and sank the ship at 17:25 hours. While the Germans were buoyed by the success, the need to launch so many sorties against a stationary vessel was a worrying portent for the future of *Küstenfliegergruppen* operations against Allied shipping.

While the naval forces at Hela had been reduced, the shore batteries proved even more problematical. On the afternoon of 5 September, *Küstenfliegergruppe* 506 was again ordered to fly a bombing raid against enemy positions. However, *Obstlt* Wolfgang von Wild, *Gruppenkommandeur* of *Küstenfliegergruppe* 506, felt this was a serious waste of resources. In the war diary for *Stab./506* appears the following entry for the evening of 5 September 1939:

CO of K.Fl.Gr.506 repeatedly informed *F.d.Luft* about his doubts concerning the planned attacks by bomber squadrons on 6.9.39. The attacks are very difficult because a relatively small target must be attacked from low-level. The attacking crews will meet very heavy flak (ten heavy AA batteries and up to thirty to forty AA machine-guns). 'Til now, 50 tons of bombs were aimed at this battery, of which 20 tons were SC500 bombs without any visible result. The planned attacks seemed to be irresponsible taking into the consideration that the target is protected by strong AA defence. It would be a waste of ammunition, especially when the planned attack on Westerplatte had been turned down for this very same reason (saving of ammunition). It had been suggested that the battery should be shelled by Schleswig-Holstein, because according to F.d.M., now the battleship could be effectively protected against mines and submarines. Unfortunately, the attack order was not cancelled, and finally, following attacks were scheduled: 3./506 morning and dusk attack, 4./186 attack at 1200 hrs.

Unable to prevent his crews from yet another operation over Hel, the following day, eight aircraft of 3./506 were launched at 02:45 hours. The original intention had been for ten aircraft, but M7+WL and M7+VL both aborted the operation with engine failure. Von Wild had been right to question the wisdom of the operation; only seven aircraft returned. From an altitude of 500 m, He 59 M7+XL (WNr 2000) had been shot down by anti-aircraft fire over Hela. Neither *Lt.z.S.* Münscher nor the *Unteroffizieren* Bäcker, Fuchs, or Mux had time to abandon the aircraft before it slammed into the ground. In a rather poignant, albeit belated, assessment, the *FdL Ost* recommended the unit undertake no further action against the port.

The intensity of action undertaken by 3./506 was reflected in its combat readiness. On 7 September, the *Staffel* had only five serviceable aircraft available. This was in contrast to 1./506 with fourteen serviceable aircraft. Despite this, the two units continued to engage Polish forces along the coast while at the same time maintain a reconnaissance presence over the Danzig Bight and Baltic Sea. By the end of September, the *Gruppe* was increasingly focusing its efforts on the port of Heinsternest, although Hela continued to occupy the unit as well.

Operations in the West

While 1 and 3 *Staffeln* operated in the Danzig bay area during *Fall Weiß*, the Do 18-equipped 2 *Staffel* remained in the west flying reconnaissance and anti-submarine patrols under the direction of *Stab./KüFlGr 406*. Operating out of Hornum, the unit had the dubious distinction of losing the first German aircraft of the war to land-based British aircraft. On 8 October, the *Staffel* had been alerted for a patrol over the Skagerrak and North Sea. Flying low over the ocean, *Lt.z.S* Hans Hornkuhl (B) and his crew were intercepted by three Hudsons from 224 Squadron. Attacking immediately, Flt Lt Walmersley ('U' N7217), Flg. Off. Burton ('M' N7215), and Sgt Cargill ('Q' N7264) forced M7+UK (WNr. 732) down and the

Above and below: Two photographs depicting the funerals of two He 59 crews killed in combat. On 21 October 1939, *Oblt.z.S* Heinrich Schlicht and his crew were killed after being shot down by Hurricanes of No. 46 Squadron off Spurn Head in He 115 S4+EH. *Oblt* Emil Wodtke along with his crew failed to return from an operation in S4+BL (WNr 2081) on 6 December 1939, after flying into a radio mast at West Beckham CH Station during the early hours.

pilot was able to perform a safe ditching 25 km off Aberdeen. Circling before departing the area, the three British pilots watched as the German crew abandoned the flying boat before sinking it with gunfire. Hornkuhl, *Fw* Willi Nahe (F), *Uffz* Hermann Plunkte (hB), and *Uffz* Toni Fait (Bm) made it safely to their dinghy and were later rescued by the Danish steamer *Teddy*. The crew was later landed at Rudkøbing on the island of Langeland and interned, but released on 25 October.

As part of the general reorganisation of the *Küstenfliegerstaffeln*, on 22 October 1939 2./506 was redesignated 1./406 and in turn replaced by a completely new unit, which was raised at List. Unlike its previous incarnation, the new unit was now equipped with the more adequate He 115 seaplane. Throughout the winter of 1939-40, operations were limited, primarily due to the intensity of the winter, yet by mid-March the *Staffel* had again begun flying more regularly. Increasingly, these operations focused upon the mining of sea lanes and estuaries in and around Britain.

In September 1939, neither the *Kriegsmarine* nor the *Luftwaffe* had any concrete plans as to how they would engage British shipping in the North Sea or along the British coastline. By November, a small number of LMA (250 kg) and LMB (945 kg) mines were available. Unlike previous contact mines, these were activated by the magnetic field of passing ships. As a result, on 5 November the decision was taken to employ these weapons in conjunction with the submarine and destroyer operations launched on 17 October. Initially, the Thames and Humber estuaries were seen as the most ideal location to focus the mining campaign, yet only *Küstenfliegergruppe* 106 3./506 (which had re-deployed to Norderney on 28 February) and 3./906 were equipped with aircraft capable of deploying the weapon. Between 20 November and 7 December, sixty-eight mines were deployed over the course of six operations, but with the onset of winter, operations were cancelled. The power struggle between the Navy and the Air Force over the deployment of the weapons meant that it was not until April that the campaign was restarted. On the night of 17/18 April, ten He 115s of 3./506 flew to the Thames estuary. By 3 May, a total of 188 mines had been deployed in the course of six operations by a variety of units. However, improved British defences precluded any German success. By September, the use of magnetic mines was discontinued in favour of the more successful acoustic versions.

Operations in Norway

On 9 April 1940, the Germans launched *Unternehmen Weserübung*, the joint invasion of Denmark and Norway. With the early capture of the

Norwegian town of Trondheim on the opening day of the campaign, both 2 and 3./506 transferred there in support of operations further north. The intended plan was for the two *Staffeln* to operate in a reconnaissance role in the North and Norwegian Seas screening for any British response by the Royal Navy. During the morning of the invasion, 1 and 2./506 both launched ten sorties each to cover the area between Bergen and the Orkneys. At shortly before 09:00 hours, the 1./506 crew of S4+CK reported three cruisers and fifteen destroyers to the south-west of Bergen, heading east. This was confirmed at 0910 when S4+DK reported more British naval units north of Bergen.

Throughout the day, the *Gruppe* was constantly engaged in reconnaissance operations. While the majority of sightings were naval, at 13:30 hours an unidentified 2./506 He 115 engaged Wing Commander

With the need for secrecy whilst engaged in mining operations along the British coastline, aircraft increasingly sported different styles of temporary camouflage. Here a He 115 of 3./506 wears night camouflage that discoloured the underwing surfaces, and national and unit markings on the fuselage. Only the individual aircraft letter remains clearly visible.

Davis in Short Sunderland 'C' N9044 of 204 Squadron. While Davis had been earlier intercepted by an Arado flown off from the Admiral Hipper, he had escaped. However, the more maneuverable and quicker He 115 was able to engage the Sunderland. While the German crew inflicted some damage on the British flying boat, the return fire from Davis' gunners left a heavy trail of smoke streaming from the Heinkel's port engine. By the time the crew returned to Trondheim, the starboard wing and engine were aflame. While the crew successfully force landed and evacuated the aircraft, it burnt out and sank shortly thereafter. While this was the *Gruppe*'s only loss of the day, a similarly unidentified He 115 of 1./506, flown by *Hptm* Wiesand, was damaged by Norwegian gunfire during the day. Meanwhile, in the north of Norway the Germans found themselves faced with a tactically disadvantageous situation. At Narvik, German ground and naval forces were without adequate air support and the British were soon to capitalise upon this.

Located some 1,500 km from Germany, the German forces in Narvik were in an unenviable position. With no adequate air support, the only meaningful maritime reconnaissance reports the garrison commander *Konteradmiral* Friedrich Bonte could rely upon was provided by U-boats. However, plagued by torpedo faults, these were in no position to provide any adequate support. On the evening of 9 April, a force of five British destroyers slipped into Ofot Fjord and engaged the German naval forces there. While 1 and 2./506 had been given over to X *Fliegerkorps* in an attempt to provide some tactical flexibility, the distance between Narvik and Trondheim precluded any meaningful deployment in defence of Bonte's forces. While the Germans were able to score some success against the British destroyer squadron, it soon proved mute when, in what became known as the Second Battle of Narvik, on 12 April, the British returned in force and sunk or critically damaged the remaining German naval forces in the region.

The loss of half of the *Kriegsmarine*'s destroyers at Narvik placed a huge strain on the ground forces in the region and brought with it an increased need to transfer air units farther north. However, a counter-invasion by Allied forces above and below Trondheim on 16 April severely restricted the *Gruppe*'s ability to support anything but the immediate needs of the local area. Meanwhile, with the 1 and 2 *Staffeln* engaged in operations in Norway, 3./506, located at Norderney, was constantly engaged in reconnaissance and mining operations along the east coast of Britain. By 3 May, it was evident that the British were withdrawing from central Norway after a reconnaissance by both 1 and 2./506 located a British force of four cruisers and nine destroyers heading at high speed in a westerly direction. A later report indicated that a battleship, a heavy and light cruiser, and up to ten destroyers were fleeing in a similar manner. However, the damage had by now already been done. Although resistance in Norway continued throughout May, as the gains made in southern and central Norway were consolidated by German forces, operations over the North increasingly wore down Norwegian defensive positions. Yet, the fact could not be ignored that despite the immediate transfer of 1 and 2./506 to Trondheim on the opening day of the campaign, the *Kriegsmarine* had suffered irreparable losses in and around Narvik through want of adequate air cover. Despite the overall success of the campaign, the inability to intervene in either the First or Second Battle of Narvik did not augur well for either *Küstenfliegergruppe* 506 specifically or German maritime air forces in general.

A Lucky Escape

With the campaign in Norway winding down by early June, operations again began to focus more on maritime reconnaissance over the North Sea. On 9 June, *Lt.z.S* Rembert van Delden (B), *Fw* Augustat (F), and *Uffz* Willi Schönfelder (Bf) took off on a patrol that shadowed the coast of Norway around Narvik. Two hours into the flight, the crew sighted a withdrawing force of British vessels abandoning positions in the Narvik area. Reporting the force, the crew continued north, where an hour later they found the British battleship HMS *Valiant* escorted by several destroyers. Unbeknownst to van Delden, earlier British sightings of German aircraft had prompted a call for air support from the nearby aircraft carrier HMS *Ark Royal*. Focusing on the battleship, none of the crew of S4+EH noticed the approach of a flight of Skuas. Sighting them too late, the radio operator Schöfelder cried out a warning and fired off a few rounds of his machine gun before he was hit by a blast of machine gun fire in the left shoulder and arm. Momentarily disorientated, Schönfelder was soon able to send out a distress signal while Augustat threw the floatplane around the sky in a desperate attempt to flee the attackers. Unable to maintain the pursuit, the British withdrew. Pilot Midshipman Kearsley of 600 Squadron later recorded, 'Skua L3024, 6Q, patrolling Valiant, at 20:00 discovered Heinkel 115 shadowing ship, opened fire at 300 yards, saw panel fall off, tail-gunner ceasing fire, total time airborne 4 hours.' While neither Kearsley or his gunner Airman Eccleshall believed they had shot the seaplane down, their attack had severely damaged the German aircraft.

With the controls to the starboard engine shot away, *Fw* Augustat struggled with the aircraft while van Delden bandaged Schöfelder's

On 9 June 1940 *Oblt* 'Pitt' Midderhoff, flying a He 115, rescued *Lt.z.S* Rembert van Delden (B), *Fw* Augustat (F) and *Uffz* Willi Schönfeld (Bf) after they were shot down by Skuas from HMS *Ark Royal* in He 115 S4+EH. Ground crew work on replacing the damaged propeller blades after this daring rescue.

wounds as best he could. With most of the flight instruments unserviceable, the pilot was forced to rely upon van Delden's use of a sextant to plot a course to Trondheim. Yet with reduced power and low fuel, after an hour he was forced to perform an emergency landing at sea. Although in the process of ditching the starboard float was torn away, the plane remained afloat. Abandoning the aircraft for their dinghy, a short while later a He 115 of 1./506 hove in to view. At the controls was *Oblt* 'Pitt' Midderhof, an experienced rescue pilot. However, Midderhof faced a raising swell, which once alighted on the sea, swamped his aircraft. The repeated crash of waves against the propellers badly bent them, but fortunately for both of the crews, the aircraft remained airworthy and Midderhof was able to take off and return to Trondheim. Eventually, S4+EH slipped beneath the waves and settled on the sea bed in position 64°50′ N 07°40′ E, where it was discovered in 1985 by surveyors working for an oil company. Willi Schönfelder, van Delden, and the British pilot Robert Kearsley all survived the war, although van Delden was a PoW after being sunk while aboard U-131 on 17 December 1941, north-east of Madeira, Portugal, in position 34°12′ N 13°35′ W. U-131 was sunk by a combination of depth charges and gunfire from the British escort destroyers HMS *Exmoor, Blankney,* and *Stanley,* the British corvette HMS *Pentstemon,* and the British sloop

HMS *Stork,* as well as gunfire from Martlet aircraft of 802 Squadron, flown off the escort carrier HMS *Audacity*. At the time, van Delden was the 1 Watch Officer.

Torpedo Operations

By August, it was becoming increasingly clear for the need to not just report upon but also attack British merchant shipping. On 23 August, the *Gruppe* had a major success when it attacked convoy OA.203 in the Firth of Moray and sank the freighters *Llanishen* (5,053 tons) and *Makaila* (6,677 tons), while damaging the motor vessel *Beacon Grange* (10,119 tons). Three days later, convoy HX.65A was target off Kinnaird Head, this time sinking the freighter *Remuera* (11,445 tons) with a torpedo. The success of these operations meant that during the early part of September 1940 five aircraft of 1./506 were adapted to carry torpedoes, while four others (S4+AH, S4+FH, and two others) retained the ability to carry bombs. While the supply of torpedoes was still slow in reaching front line units, there were sufficient stocks available for small scale operations. However, the successes achieved by the *Gruppe* belied the dangers inherent in such operations. On 15 September, 3./506 was alerted for an attack on a large tanker that reconnaissance flights during the day had located sailing south from the Firth of Moray. Late that evening, two aircraft took off in an attempt to relocate and attack the vessel. At approximately 23:00 hours, the crew of S4+CL (WNr 3261), *Oblt* Clement Lucas (F), *Hptm* Ernst-Welhelm Bergmann (B), *Fw* Ernst Kalinowski (Bf), and *Hptm* Hans Kriependorf (h.B), sighted the British ship accompanied by the convoy escort vessel HMS *Vortigen*. Circling to attack the ship, Lucas came in from the south-west. He later reported:

> In case of anti-aircraft fire, we attacked at low-level. About 500 m ahead of the ship, I climbed to 50 m, aimed at the middle of the ship using my night sights as well as an angle allowance, pressed the button on the right of my control column and released the torpedo.

So as not to affect the course of the torpedo with the slipstream, Lucas then flew straight ahead for 30 seconds, observing, 'The tanker had been hit amidships.' However, the inability to alter course after releasing the torpedo meant Lucas now flew directly over the convoy and was engaged by the ships' anti-aircraft fire. In the hail of defensive fire, both of the Heinkel's engines were hit. Unable to maintain height, Lucas was forced to make an emergency landing without any problems. Lucas later recalled,

'It was 00:35 hrs in the morning of 16 September. Our Bordfunker
[Kalinowski] fixed a drogue anchor to both floats to stabilise the plane.
When two small, grey fishing boats appeared at about 04:00 hours, we
scuttled the aircraft.' However, the attempt to destroy the aircraft was
unsuccessful, as it merely turned turtle. The approaching fisherman rescued
Lucas, and his crew attached a tow cable to the stricken aircraft and towed
it to Eyemouth where it was beached. While Lucas claimed to have hit a
tanker, the only damage to shipping done that night was the sinking of
Swedish steamer *Holland*, which was making a northerly course as part
of FN79. Aside from the loss of S4+CH and its crew, *Küstenfliegergruppe*
506 suffered a double blow as *Hptm* Bergmann was the *Staffelkapitän*
of 3./506, while *Hptm* Kriependorf was the *Staffelkapitän* of 1./506.
Apparently, Kriependorf had requested to accompany the operation to
gain experience in torpedo attacks against merchant shipping. The loss of
such experienced men as Lucas, Bergmann, and Kriependorf was hammer-
blow for both 1 and 3./506, which suspended torpedo operations for the
next five days. Yet, by 21 September both units were back in action against
shipping, this time a reported convoy consisting of twenty-four medium-
sized steamers. Again, the lack of torpedo stocks meant only two aircraft
from each unit (S4+AH and EH of 1./506, and S4+GL and HL of 3./506)
could participate. While the four crews successfully located the convoy
near Kinnaird Head, none were able to score a success.

Sometimes He 115 aircraft were employed as transports. Here S4+DH of 1./506
ferries in a new float as a replacement for another aircraft.

On 11 November, 2./506 scored another spectacular result. Briefed the previous evening for an armed reconnaissance of the British coast, several aircraft had flown single sortie operations in search of a reported convoy heading north-west, south of Hartlepool. The returning S4+DK of *Oblt. z.S* Bungards had located the convoy consisting of approximately twenty ships in a double line and protected by destroyers and escort vessels. While his first attack on a tanker was thwarted by defensive fire from a destroyer, Bungards fired his torpedo at a freighter he estimated to be about 6,000 tons. While he believed his aim had been flawless, Bungards later claimed his torpedo had not run true and as a result had not scored a hit. Meanwhile, *Oblt.z.S* Ralf Münnich had taken off from Norderney at 21:45 hours at the controls of S4+GK to attack shipping in the same area. At 00:25 hours (BST) Münnich came across a small convoy heading west and attacked. His observer, *Lt.z.S* Haude, later reported they had torpedoed a freighter they believed to be about 6,000 to 8,000 tons. He continued, 'After torpedo explosion, unusually high second explosion, after which the steamer broke in two and immediately sank.' Postwar research would indicate the ship Haude had sunk was the Norwegian vessel the *Ravnanger*, which was registered as 3,371GRT. It had sailed from Middlesbrough in ballast and was scheduled to become part of convoy FN330. It was sunk approximately 2-km north-east of No. 20 buoy, Tees Bay. The only casualty was the 3rd Engineer Ola Karlsen. Like the *Ravnanger*, S4+GK was soon also destroyed. While making his landing approach at Zwischenahn, a technical failure developed in the Heinkel (WNr 2786) and Münnich was unable to land safely. In the subsequent crash, Münnich was slightly injured, but S4+DK was completely written off.

While operations against shipping continued, as the weather deteriorated with the onset of winter operations became increasingly more infrequent. On 13 November, 2./506 was notified that its current *Staffelkapitän Maj.* Wolfgang von Zezschwitz was to be transferred to *Generalstab* training at the *Luftkriegsakademie* Berlin-Gatow. He was to be replaced by *Hptm* Thomsen, who was already a member of the *Staffel*.

Weather Reconnaissance

With the fall of Norway in June 1940, the Germans established long-range meteorological reconnaissance units to monitor weather cells over the North and Arctic Seas and the Northern Atlantic Ocean. Until September, the Norwegian weather station on Jan Mayen had continued to transmit weather reports. However, these ceased on 3 September, and so it was decided that Dr Erich Etienee, Arctic consultant of *Luftflotte* 5, would make a survey of the island to establish whether or not a German-operated weather station could be set up there. With the geography of the island precluding a land-based operation, on 12 September He 115 S4+BK of 2./506, flown by *Oblt* Heydt, took off at 04:30 hours from Tromsø. Aside from Heydt, the crew consisted of *Lt* Müller (B), *Fw* Hundertmark (Bf), and Etienne. After 6 hours and despite a heavy swell, the crew landed near Eggøya. For the next 3 hours, Etienne explored the area, before leaving at 13:20 hours for the return trip to Norway. Landing at 19:30 hours, the reconnaissance operation was considered successful and the decision was taken to set up a German-operated weather station on the island.

Buoyed by the success of the 12 September operation, five days later a further weather reconnaissance operation was undertaken. This time, Etienne took off for Kapp Linné on the south coast of Spitsbergen. Accompanying *Fw* Porella (F), *Oblt* Bierich, and *Oblt* Burmester, Etienne took off at 05:00 hours from Tromsø. 3 hours and 21 minutes later, *Oblt* Heydt was again airborne in S4+BK, this time headed to the Soviet-manned station at Barentsburg in Grønfjord. While Heydt found the Soviets unwilling to cooperate, Etienne had a more successful time. At 12:54 hours, S4+BK lifted off on its return journey, followed 6 minutes later by Etienne in the second seaplane. While Heydt returned to Tromsø

He 115 S4+HH of 1./506 banks away towards the coast during a routine patrol in 1940.

at 18:56 hours, Etienne's Heinkel encountered heavy winds on the return journey, which delayed its arrival in Norway until 20:05 hours.

While the unit continued at irregular intervals to assist meteorological operations in the region, increasingly the burden fell to *Küstenfliegergruppen* 406 and 906. With the introduction of the Bv 138 to these *Gruppen*, the extra endurance provided by the more economical diesel engines proved more valuable to meteorological operations than the more conventional petrol-driven engines of *KüFlGr* 506's Ju 88s. As a result, by early 1941 operations of this kind had all but ceased.

1941

Following the award of the *Ritterkreuz* to *Oblt* Karl Barth of 3./506 on 14 December 1940, the various *Staffeln* of the *Gruppe* underwent a period of reorganisation. In early 1941, 1./506 began converting to the Junkers Ju 88 land-based bomber. Located at Perleberg, the united had completed its conversion by March and maintained a consistently high operational readiness with an average of nine serviceable aircraft (from a total of eleven) and a similar ratio of crews by early April. Meanwhile, the chronic shortage of torpedoes continued to hamper operations. On average, 3./506 had a stock of five pieces throughout the period. However, this did not preclude armed reconnaissance off the north-east coast of Britain between 52° N and 58° N. Increasingly, operations by all three *Staffeln* encountered patrolling British aircraft, usually identified as Blenheims. The improvement in Allied patrols and defensive armament aboard ships moved the *Führer der Luftstrietkräfte* to order that operations over the North Sea, particularly close to the British coastline, were henceforth only to be conducted with favourable cloud cover or moonlight conditions. If these were absent then the *Gruppe*'s pilots were instructed to abort their operations. The reason for this was soon evident. After a patrol on 25 April, *Lt* Staffehl (1./506) reported unusual night-fighter activity to Kinnaird Head, while defensive fire from an escort vessel attacked by *Lt* Immenroth of the same *Staffel* the day after put the hydraulic system and flaps out of action on S4+LH. Despite this, 1./506 particularly was still able to inflict meaningful damage on North Sea shipping, albeit at an increasing risk. On 28 April, *Lt* Stähler (B) of S4+CH claimed an attack on a convoy while the crew of *Lt* Adolph (B) in S4+GH successfully intercepted a steamer the same night. Yet the writing was on the wall for the He 115-equipped *Staffeln*. On 29 April, the Stab./506 war diary noted that increasing confrontations with enemy aircraft 'compel the changeover of 3./506 to the Ju 88 as soon as possible, particularly in relation to the torpedo situation'. However, not even the Ju 88s were immune to defensive fire from the British. The following day, *Gfr* Alfred Schmiegel (Bs) was killed after his compartment was hit by defensive fire from ships that S4+DH had been attacking. A later report by the observer *Lt* Paul Dreher noted:

> After defensive fire from a destroyer or an auxiliary cruiser, dropped two 500-kg bombs at a not precisely defined target. During attack there was heavy and accurate defensive fire from light flak. As we turned away, there was heavy flak on both sides. Result of bombing not observed because the rear gunner was killed. Shortly after dropping the bombs there was the first hits on the aircraft – in the cockpit and gondola. *Gefr* Schmiegel had an artery severed in his right thigh. Not possible to lift him out. Bled to death.

Dreher was similarly wounded, suffering flesh wounds to his right hand and losing his little finger. On the same night, S4+HH (Wnr 0715) was shot down during a reconnaissance sortie between 54°30' N and 55°30' N. While the body of *Hptgfr* Josef Schumacher (Bs) later washed ashore on 10 June, the remainder of the crew, *Lt* Hans Jark (B), *Fw* Kurt Pahnke (F), and *Uffz* Johann Schaare (Bf), were never found. The following day, S4+FH (Wnr 0711) failed to return from an armed reconnaissance operation to the English coast. Aboard were *Oblt* Werner Beck (B), *Obfw*

S4+LH taxies out in preparation for a fateful sortie.

Stefan Haberkern (F), *Fw* Wilhelm Schwarz (Bf), and *Ogfr* Arthur Wagner (Bs).

At the beginning of May, 1./506 had eleven observers on strength: *Hptm* Sched, *Oblt* Beck (MIA 2.5.41), Pehl (MIA 26.5.44), *Ltn* Adolph, Dreher, Immenroth, Sieber, Staffehl, Stähler, and Rupp. However, Dreher's injury and the loss of Beck so early in the month placed an increased strain on the remaining officers in the unit. While Dreher would return to active duty, his recuperation took many weeks. Perhaps due to these losses, on 3 May the *Staffel* was order by *Gruppe Nord* that dropping bombs on alternative land targets was henceforth forbidden. Only in an emergency was the bombing of land-targets permissible, and the *Gruppe* was again reminded that if cloud cover was unavailable west of 04° E, operations were to be aborted.

Despite the setbacks, the unit continued to engage shipping, specifically targeting all fishing boats encountered westwards of 03° E. On 11 May, the *Gruppe* participated in a combined air and sea operation against shipping in the mid-North Sea. Throughout the course of the day, 3./506 observed about 130 fishing vessels that were either intercepted or closely reconnoitered. Danish fishing vessels of the period were particularly affected by air operations of both sides. While close to Danish waters, the RAF often attacked them, while if they strayed too far out too sea, the Germans intercepted them. At the end of May, 3./506 was ordered to

The nose of a 2./506 He 115 clearly showing the later version of the unit's insignia – a roaring tiger's head.

transfer to Westerland to join 1./506. Here, the unit would begin the slow conversion to the Ju 88, though in the meantime, sorties along the British coastline continued.

With the opening of the Russian campaign and the quick gaining of territory in the Baltic, it became necessary to transfer air units to the region. As a result, on 21 September both 1 and 3./506 transferred to Riga under the overall command of *Fliegerführer Ostsee* [*Stab./906*]. The move by 1./506 was made more difficult, as for the two days 18-19 September, five of its Ju 88s – S4+HL (WNr 1077), S4+LL (WNr 1099), S4+AL (WNr 1045), S4+HL (WNr 1144), and S4+ML (WNr 1323) – suffered technical problems that kept them grounded. Despite this, the *Gruppe* managed to undertake continuous operations against the Russian garrison on Saaremaa (Ösel) off the Estonian west coast. While the operation was quickly and successfully concluded, the increasing need for land-based bombers by the *Luftwaffe* in support of the land war meant there was little chance 1 and 3./506 would return to the west in operations against Allied shipping. The move towards a more land-based focus was all but confirmed on 6 October when the final seaplane-equipped *Staffel*, 2./506, transferred to Westerland for conversion to the Ju 88. Then, on 19 October 1941 *Küstenfliegergruppe 506* was redesignated as *Kampfgruppe 506* and henceforth dropped all maritime pretence. While the *Gruppe* had returned to the west by the close of 1941, its association with the *Kriegsmarine* was no more, and it increasingly identified itself as a bomber unit and not a coastal reconnaissance group.

9

Küstenfliegergruppe 606

In mid-September 1938, the general reorganisation of the *Küstenfliegerstaffeln* saw the creation of a new *Staffel*. While it was intended the *Staffel* would in time be supplemented by two others and a *Stab*, thereby becoming a complete *Gruppe*, for over a year 2./ *Küstenfliegerstaffel* 606 remained the sole representative of the planned unit. The new *Staffel* was created rather than raised by the renumbering of the 2./706. Based at Kamp and equipped with the Dornier Do 18, the *Staffel* was commanded by *Hptm* Rudolf Wodarg. As with all pre-war *Staffeln*, the unit operated regularly in over-water reconnaissance and search and rescue operations.

The War Effort

With the outbreak of hostilities on 1 September 1939, 2./606 was transferred from its base at Kamp to new quarters at List. From here, it was intended that the unit would be under the command of *Stab./306*, itself subordinate to *Führer der Luftstrietkräfte West*. Its *Staffelkapitän* had since been changed to *Hptm* Hans-Bruno von Laue. The primary responsibility for the *Staffel* would be long-range reconnaissance of the North Sea. Included in this brief was anti-submarine warfare. It was during such an operation on 7 September that the *Staffel* suffered its first war-time loss.

During mid-afternoon of 7 September, 2./606 had launched a series of reconnaissance sorties over the lower North Sea region. Each Do 18 had been armed with SC250 bombs. At around 17:00 hours, 8L+WK (WNr 0833), crewed by *Oblt.z.S* Rabbach (B), *Uffz* Ernst Hinrichs (F), *Uffz* Evers

(Bm), and *OGfr* Rusch (Hilf.B), saw a submerging submarine. Rolling in for an attack, the crew soon realised their intended victim was in fact a German u-boat. Fortunately, the attack was called off and no damage was caused to the submerging boat. Yet the fateful flight of 8L+WK was far from over. Upon returning to base, the pilot Hinrichs fouled his landing approach, touching down at too great a speed and causing the aircraft to overturn. In the accident, the aircraft was completely destroyed, while Rabbach and Evers were both killed and Rusch was slightly injured. Hinrichs himself was heavily injured in the accident.

Pace of operations over the North Sea continued throughout September. Occasionally, German crews would cross paths with British aircraft involved in similar reconnaissance operations. On 19 September, Do 18 8L+EK encountered an Avro Anson of 612 Squadron 196 km (122 miles) east of Wick. Turning to engage the German flying boat, the Anson was

Do 18 60+X62 of 2./606 at its moorings in the pre-war days. Only the 2 *Staffel* was raised as a maritime unit.

able to make four firing passes before 8L+EK was able to escape into cloud having sustained no damage. The following day, the British Home Fleet put to sea in an effort to support one of its damaged submarines attempting to make safe harbour. In the meantime, the *Oberkommando der Marine* had ordered a comprehensive search for the fleet by eighteen long-range Do 18s from 3./306, 2./506, and 2./606; the latter supplied six aircraft for the operation. It was the reconnaissance of this operation that led to the large-scale attack later in the day by He 111s of 1./KG 26 and the newly introduced Ju 88As of I./KG 30, which attributed the apparent sinking of the British carrier HMS *Ark Royal* to *Gfr* Carl Francke.

The excitement created by the operations against the Home Fleet soon dissipated, as on 17 October the *Staffel* suffered another loss. During mid-morning, the unit had been alerted to undertake a search and rescue operation for a crew of a missing Ju 88 belonging to 2./KG 30. Part of this force was Do 18 8L+DK (WNr 0809), crewed by *Oblt.z.S* Siegfried Saloga (B), *Fw* Paul Grabbet (F), *Uffz* Kurt Seydel (Bm), and *Oberfunkmaat* Hilmar Grim (Bf). At around 13:30 hours, when 40-km (25 miles) east of Berwick, the aircraft was engaged by Gladiators from B Flight, 607 Squadron. The British pilots, Flt Lt John Sample, Flg. Off. G.D. Craig, and Plt Off. W. H. Whitley, made several passes on the Dornier, which inflicted considerable damage. Although Grabbet was able to keep the Dornier aloft for another 30 minutes after the Gladiators withdrew, he was forced to ditch the aircraft some 30 km (27 miles) away. In the attempt to ditch, the aircraft stalled as it flared for touch-down and crashed. Although the radio-operator Grimm was unwounded, both Grabbet and Saloga were injured, while the mechanic Kurt Seydel was killed. The three survivors were later rescued by the Polish destroyer ORP *Grom* and interned.

Reorganisation, Redesignation, and Controversy

The reorganisation of the *Küstenfliegergruppen* in late October 1939 brought serious changes to the type and employment of hitherto maritime aircraft-equipped units and the role they were expected to play. As of 22 October 1939, the 2 *Staffel* was renamed as the 2 *Staffel* of the newly formed *Küstenfliegergruppe* 906. With no other units associated with the *Gruppe*, the decision was taken to only reform the *Staffel* on 1 November at Kiel-Holtenau. However, the *Staffel* was to be an entirely new unit raised from scratch. In addition, the *Staffel* was to be supplemented by a 1, 3, and *Stabsstaffel*, thereby creating a completely new *Küstenfliegergruppe*.

Originally, the intention had been to reform the *Gruppe* as a dedicated naval aviation unit. However, the comprehensive reorganisation order

Above and opposite: A sequence of pictures showing a wartime Do 18 returning from patrol in 1939.

directed that *KüFlGr* 606 should begin conversion to the Do 17 effective 1 November. This departure from maritime aviation was signalled in the orders that stipulated the *Gruppe* was henceforth to consider its deployment and training as that of a land-based *Kampfgruppe*. During early November 1939, very shortly after their assemblage at Kamp the new units were transferred to Kiel-Holtenau, where they began equipping with and training on the Do 17. From November 1939 until April 1940, the *Gruppe* began working up in preparation for offensive operations against the west. During the period of its working up, the new *Gruppe* was under the command of *Obstlt* Hermann Edert.

Edert had been the *Gruppenkommandeur* of *Küstenfliegergruppe* 706 prior to its redesignation during October 1939 (and his reassignment as *Gruppenkommandeur*) as *Küstenfliegergruppe* 906, so he was no stranger to command assignments. However, by July 1940 Edert had been replaced and *Maj.* Joachim Hahn had been placed in command, thus sealing the fate of the unit as a land-orientated *Kampfgruppe*. An intelligence report compiled in early November 1940 noted of the unit:

The Group Commander is *Maj*. Hahn, a man of forceful personality, about thirty-five years old. He insists on carrying on with his own ideas, even though these are not always approved either by his superiors or other members of the Group. He is nevertheless popular in the Group; his courage and human qualities are much admired. *Maj*. Hahn is a great believer in very low-level formation attacks and is insisting on his Group carrying out these tactics, especially when attacking aerodromes. On occasion, attacks are said to have been carried out from as low as 30 feet, and crews thoroughly dislike the idea, as they invariably meet with severe opposition from the ground defences. The first time this tactic was employed was during an attack on St Eval Aerodrome early in October [1940]. *Maj*. Hahn flew in 7T+AA and was accompanied only by the *Staffel Kapitane* of 2 and 3 *Staffeln* in their own aircraft. While the raid was thought to be successful, all aircraft were badly damaged. Shortly after this raid, a second raid was carried out on Penrose by three aircraft of 1./606. On this raid, 7T+CH failed to return.

It was thought that originally the Group had been intended re-equip with He 111s, but *Maj*. Hahn fought against this on the grounds he considered the aircraft unsuitable for coastal work, so the unit received

Do 17s instead. At all times, one Do 17 is kept solely for coastal and anti-shipping work. In 1./606, 7T+CH is this aircraft. Three men are employed at all times as painters in maintaining the aircraft's finish. There is a difficulty with the Group in that it carries out both land-based attacks as well as attacks on shipping. For attacks on land, KFlGr 606 is under the command of *Fl.Korps* IV, while attacks on shipping are overseen by *Marine Gruppe West*. This obviously creates command problems. As a result of a fiery speech by Göring concerning the raising of London, *Maj.* Hahn usually refers to the judgment of Fl.Korps IV.

Tactics against shipping were: to fly diagonally across the path of the ship and drop a trial bomb; then make a 180° and come in on a second approach and drop two bombs. Pilot then turned through 225° to drop two more bombs along the length of the ship. SC 50 bombs were normally carried on these armed reconnaissance flights. If the attack were carried out from a low altitude, such as 300 feet, bombs would be released purely by judgment. The alternative height was 3,000 feet, when the bombsight would be used. In the case of zig-zag avoiding action by the ship, the aircraft would attack immediately the ship came back on its original course.

10

Küstenfliegergruppe 706

In July 1937, a reorganisation and expansion of coastal air units saw the creation of the first *Staffel* of what would become *Küstenfliegergruppe 706*. This new unit was created by renumbering 1./406 as 1./706. In addition, 2./706 was formed from scratch. These two units developed along familiar patterns already established in other *Gruppen*. Then, in October 1937, as part of the expansion of naval air forces, a *Stabsstaffel* was created for the *Gruppe*. One of the new members of the *Gruppe* was Günther Krech. Born in 1914, Krech had joined the Navy in 1933. Upon being commissioned a *Leutnant zur See* in October 1936, he transferred to 1./106 as an observer before being transferred to 1./706 in October 1937 and finally ending his aviation career in *KüFlGr* 506. Krech would ultimately end the war as a prisoner of war, although he was responsible for sinking seventeen merchant vessels, two war ships, and damaging three tankers.

Arguably the most erratic in its formation, disbandment, reforming, and operational history, in September 1938 2./706 was redesignated as 2./606. It would not be until June 1943 that the unit was reformed, and then only for a month. This left just one combat *Staffel*, 1./706, and the *Stab./706* as the sole representatives of the *Gruppe*. Then in November 1938, 3./706 was raised at Kamp operating the He 59. This represented the limit of cohesiveness that the *Gruppe* ever achieved. With the outbreak of war in September 1939, *Obstlt* Hermann Edert, the *Gruppe*'s commander, instructed his crews that prior to the official announcement on 3 September, British and French aircraft could be engaged along with any Polish forces encountered in the Danzig Bight area. This aggressiveness was reflected by the aircrews, and brought success on 4 September when the *Staffelkapitän* of 3./706, *Hptm* Gerd Stein, landed the fatal blow and sunk the Polish mine-layer ORP *Gryf*. Not content with this success, the Germans cast

The emblem of the longest serving
Staffel in the *Gruppe*, 1./706.

about for further ways of restricting merchant shipping and combating
the enemy at sea.

Operating against Polish forces, the *Staffel* was in constant action for
the first weeks of the war. However, the need to remain focused on the
war on mercantile trade left many wondering what options were available
to the *Gruppe*. On 16 September 1939, it was suggested that in order
to intensify the trade war on shipping, two boarding commandos, each
consisting of an officer, radioman, and one or two soldiers, should be
formed using observers and ground personnel from 1./706. It was intended
that these raiding parties would accompany operations by He 59s, and
when a merchant vessel suspected of carrying contraband was sighted, the
aircraft would land close by and the boarding parties would go aboard.
Discussions had specifically noted the He 59 as the perfect aircraft type
for such operations, as it had good handling characteristics, low landing
speeds, could operate in slight swells, and had space aboard for the extra
men. In addition, it could carry a useful bomb load. It was decided that
the procedure for such operations would entail two aircraft working in
tandem. One He 59 would send a request to the suspicious ship to heave to
and lower a boat ready for what the Germans termed a frisk action. It was
expected that all the ship's key documents were to be ready for inspection.
Thus, while one aircraft landed to disembark its boarding commando, the
second would stay airborne as a protective watch. If the ship was found

to be carrying contraband it was to be escorted to Swinemünde. While the proposal was accepted, it was noted that those soldiers tasked with such duties needed specialised training by legal experts on the subject of 'boarding' law. While these proposals were being developed, 3./706 took delivery of three new He 115s to begin operational work alongside the older He 59s. However, the *Gruppe* did not have things all its own way. On 9 October 1939, He 59 P5+HL (WNr 1996) of 3./706 crashed into the sea near Sylt during an operational patrol, killing all aboard. Such patrols were conducted in fan-like patterns. These operations constituted the bulk of operations conducted by the unit in the early months of the war.

With the war against Poland coming to an end, it became obvious that the variously scattered *Küstenfliegerstaffeln* should be reorganised to better facilitate communication between combat units and their respective *Stabsstafeln*. Consequently, in October the general reorganisation of naval air units saw the *Stab*, 1, and 3 *Staffeln* renamed as the *Stab*, 1, and 3 *Staffeln* of an entirely new *Gruppe* numbered 906. Thus, *Küstenfliegergruppe* 706

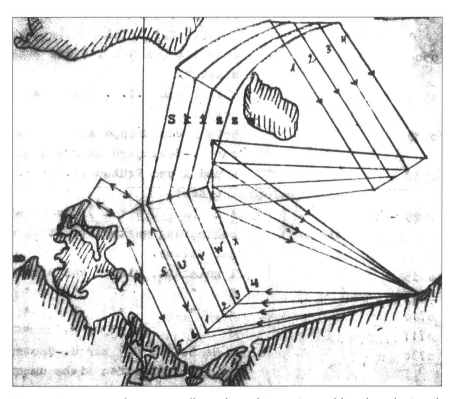

Reconnaissance patrols were usually performed in sections, although each aircraft flew an individual path just beyond visual range of the others on the operation. This allowed for the maximum search area to be covered at any given time.

ceased to exist. However, late in 1939 the decision was taken to rebuild the *Gruppe*, and on 1 January 1940 1./706 was reformed at Keil-Holtenau. The initial incarnation of the *Staffel* had operated the He 60. However, the revived formation was now equipped with the He 59. For the time being, this proved the only *Staffel* of the *Gruppe* until July, when a *Stabsstaffel* was formed at Stavanger.

With the severity of the winter over 1939-40 closing down much of the German coastline due to sea ice forming in harbours, operations were heavily restricted. However, when conditions proved suitable the main duties of the *Staffel* focused on anti-submarine patrols in the Skagerrak and Kattegat, escort duties for German shipping in the region, and reconnaissance operations over the North Sea. As the sole representative of the *Gruppe*, supplies inundated the *Staffel*. On 20 April 1940, He 59 NE+TD (WNr. 1991) was taken on strength, having previously served with the transport unit *Kampfgruppe zur besonderen Verwendung* 108 in Norway. This meant that with so many aircraft, a temporary, unofficial

Two He 115s of 1./706, resting on their beaching trolleys at Aalborg-See.

2./706 was set up. The newly acquired He 59 NE+TD was assigned the combat identity of 6I+IK. This increase in operational ability greatly enhanced combat effectiveness. However, it was to be short lived. In mid-June 1940, all He 59s on strength with the two *Staffeln* were ordered transferred to the *Seenotdienst* for conversion to air-sea rescue aircraft. With this loss of aircraft, the temporary 2./706 was disbanded. At the same time, 1./706 transferred to Aalborg-See, where the unit undertook conversion training on the Ar 196 and He 115 seaplanes, although it was the latter on which most operations were to be undertaken. Acutely aware of possible inclement weather, the *Staffel* sometimes used the harbour at Thisted as a base of operations.

Often the weather at Aalborg-See was difficult. On 8 September, Ar 196 CK+FJ (WNr 0095) was heavily damaged during a storm at Aalborg-See, only reinforcing the need for an alternate base of operations at Thisted. Such misfortune was replicated on 20 September when He 59 6I+CK (WNr 2598) was damaged after hitting an obstacle during its takeoff run. While no crew losses were sustained, it did reinforce the need for vigilance. Throughout the year and into 1941, the primary focus of the unit became the Skagerrak, with much time spent on anti-submarine patrols and convoy escort duties of ships passing through the region either on their way to or from Norway. This meant the *Staffel* was rarely exposed to Allied combat aircraft, and the majority of incidents suffered by the unit were either related to mechanical failures or weather.

The limited contact with enemy air forces did not preclude the *Staffel* from aircraft and crews going missing during operational and non-operational sorties. On 13 September, Bv 138 K6+FK (WNr. 0027) was lost without a trace having taken off from Drontheim. While the body of *Ogfr* Franz Hell (Bm) was later washed ashore, *Uffz* Karl Schenker (F), *Lt* Günter Schast (B), *Gfr* Georg Heller (Bf), and *Uffz* Otto Hilger (Bm) were recorded as missing. Yet things were not always stacked against the Germans. Throughout 1940 and into 1941, the primary reason for aircraft damage proved technical; either pilots would run out of fuel and were forced to make an emergency landing, or else engine failures necessitated similar forced landings.

On 22 October 1941, the *Staffel* gained somewhat of a pyrrhic victory in the war against enemy aircraft. While on a transfer flight, a Bv 138 of *Stab./706* engaged a Catalina of No. 413 Squadron, RCAF, and shot it down off the coast of Norway. The victory was marred somewhat, as the pilot *Hptm* Johannes Gässler was injured during the combat by return fire. It appears that Gässler was the *Staffelkapitän* of 1./706 at the time of his injury. He was replaced by *Oblt* Arthur Schmidt. Meanwhile, the *Stab* was now based at Trondheim, where it had relocated in March 1941. The

Above and below: Operations by 1./706 focused primarily on the Kattegat and Skagerrak. British intelligence regularly intercepted radio traffic from aircraft on patrol or escort duties in the region. One of the primary functions was to guard against enemy submarine activity. On 11 June 1940, a patrolling aircraft photographed the wake left by a diving submarine. Almost without exception, when aircraft encountered phenomena such as this they acted, the results of which left a tell-tale mark on the surface of the ocean.

The mooring lines of a 1 *Staffel* Heinkel are checked after the completion of an operation in 1941.

move was only temporary, as in November *Stab./706* was to relocate to Tromsø, where it would stay until July 1943 when it was redesignated as *Stab./Seeaufklängsgruppe 130*.

On 20 December, 1./706 again suffered the loss of its *Staffelkapitän*, *Oblt* Arthur Schmidt. During a routine flight, the He 115 (WNr 2083) he was flying crashed after developing technical problems with the engines. The aircraft came down at Hirtshals in Denmark. *Oblt.z.S* Dietrich Steinhart (B) and *Ogfr* Norbert Vogel (Bf) were also killed. Schmidt's place in the *Staffel* was taken by *Oblt* Garlichs. With few personnel killed during the year, such a loss was difficult for the *Staffel*. Equally difficult was the worsening weather, and often operations were cancelled or recalled early, as low cloud and heavy seas precluded flying.

During 1942, operations were again expanded into the North Sea. Although this brought with it increased risk of interception, the *Staffel* remained lucky. The losses incurred were primarily as a result of technical difficulties. Consequently, high serviceability rates could be maintained. Early in March, the unit's strength stood at ten He 115s, two Ar 196s, and two Fi 156 liaison aircraft. In May, the unit traded its ten He 115 for four Bv 138s. The following month, the unit received a total of six supplementary aircraft, but had five transferred to other units. This meant the conversion to the Bv 138 was slow. As a result, operations focused

With the equipping of the Bv 138, the range of operations was extended. Here two aircraft are on patrol over a calm ocean.

A Bv 138 is prepared for an operation. Aboard the raft with the white caps, two naval officers can be seen.

mainly around short-range patrols using the Ar 196. For the remainder of its existence, the number of available Bv 138s in the *Staffel* never exceeded seven.

With the tide of the war turning, it became obvious that the *Luftwaffe* was increasingly asserting its authority. Although a last ditch effort was made to bolster the dwindling numbers of *Küstenfliegerstaffeln* with the reforming of 2./706 in Tromsø during June 1943, it was a mute point. In July, the *Stab,* 1, and 2 *Staffeln* were turned over to *Luftwaffe* control and renamed as the *Stab*, 1, and 2 *Staffeln* of *Seeaufklängsgruppen* 130. One of the last major incidents to befall the *Gruppe* occurred on 2 July; while being prepared for an operation, Bv 138 (WNr 1049) of 1./706 suffered an explosion that wrote the aircraft off. An investigation into the incident found the most likely cause was sabotage. Thus came to an end the combat career of *Küstenfliegergruppe* 706.

11

Küstenfliegergruppe 806

The general reorganisation of naval air units in October 1939 gave rise to a new *Gruppen*. By renumbering the *Stab*, 1, and 3 *Staffeln* of *Küstenfliegergruppe* 506 and 1./306, the *Stab*, 1, 2, and 3 *Staffeln* of *Küstenfliegergruppe* 806 were brought into existence. The various *Staffeln* were located Dievenow, Kamp, Brüsterort, and Kiel-Holtenau respectively. Initially equipped with seaplanes, the *Gruppen* was quickly retrained on the He 111J, a torpedo-bomber version of the Heinkel intended for anti-shipping operations, during December.

Unlike other seaplane *Küstenfliegergruppen*, the *Gruppe* was not as restricted by the winter conditions, as it was able to operate from established airfields. Despite this, the work up and conversion to the He 111 was slow to be completed. Operational losses also hampered the process. By early 1940, the *Kriegsmarine* was bemoaning the technical deficiencies of the type. It was becoming increasingly clear that the type was ill-suited to its intended purpose. On 27 November, WNr 5089 was 80 per cent damaged when it crashed due to engine failure. The difficulties encountered with the type meant that the *Gruppe* was obliged to continue using seaplanes. However, the misfortune with unreliable aircraft continued. On 9 December, *Uffz* Heinrich Pflüger (F) and *Ogfr* Friedrich Salefy (Bm) of 1./806 were killed in a flying accident when the He 114 (WNr 2567) crashed off Dievenow in bad weather. This was followed by another flying accident on 14 December when He 111J (WNr 5039) of 3./806 crashed on takeoff. However, in this instance the crew were unhurt.

In January, issues were raised about whether the conversion to the He 111J would be successfully completed before the Spring, with reports being filed that aircraft maintenance was an issue. Mid-January, 2./806 seriously considered using rail to transport two particularly temperamental

Atypical of other *Küstenfliegergruppen*, 806 was equipped with land-based aircraft. Illustrated here is the emblem of an unidentified *Staffel* from the *Gruppe* on the nose of a He 111J.

airframes to repair facilities. The main problem with the type appeared to be its DB600 power-plants. On 27 January, WNr 5076 crashed due to engine failure. The engine-related woes for the *Gruppe* continued when on 30 January *Uffz* Klawika (F), *Fl.* Schirmer (Bm), *Fl.* Grieskammer (Bf), and *Uffz* Kermbach (passenger) of 3./806 were killed in a non-operational flight when the W34 (WNr 4026) aircraft they were flying crashed from a height of 20 m soon after takeoff due to engine failure.

Despite numerous difficulties caused by the type, the unit continued its conversion process. By the beginning of February 1940, the *Gruppe* had completed its conversion and had on strength the following aircraft at Sagan-Küpper: WNrn 5046, 5057, 5058, 5064, 5070, 4075, 5076, 5083, 5163, 5189, 5197, and 5198. These were supplemented at Nordhausen by the five reserve aircraft: 5006, 5036, 5040, 5167, and 5177. Meanwhile, at Kiel-Holtenau there were the following: 5060, 5062, 5067, 5065, 5069, 5071, 5087, 5088, 5090, 5091, 5092, 5094, 5152, 5157, 5164, 5172, 5179, 5185, 5187, and 5188. These were further supplemented during the month with WNr 5180 and 5183 being transferred to the unit in the first week of February. However, it was not long before these aircraft were involved in accidents.

As with other *Küstenfliegergruppen*, the *Gruppe* was employed in armed reconnaissance of the Kattegat, Skagerrak, and east coast of Britain. On

With the conversion to the Ju 88 and *Kampfgruppe* status, the unit's emblems changed, as was necessary. Here, members of 1./KGr 806 celebrate the 2,000th operation. On the board below the nose of the cockpit can be seen the emblems used by the *Gruppe*.

10 February, 3./806 began the process of transferring to Uetersen for better access to its main patrol areas. At 10:00 hours, WNr 5180 and 5183 collided while taxiing to their respective dispersal areas. While the former suffered 35 per cent damage, the latter was written off. Despite this, the *Gruppe* began operating regular reconnaissance patrols. On 22 February, 2./806 had been ordered to send a force of seven aircraft to the east coast of England on an armed reconnaissance. Alerted by radar, Squadron Leader Fairtlough, Ft Lt Mitchell, and Plt Off. Taylor of 254 Squadron took off to intercept in their Blenheim fighters. Sighting M7+DK 160 km east of Flamborough Head, the trio engaged the Heinkel. For the next 20 minutes, the British crews traded gunfire with the gunners aboard the German aircraft. Having expended their ammunition just as the Heinkel disappeared into the mist, the British turned for home believing they had inflicted serious damage that would preclude the enemy aircraft from regaining its home base. Despite the amount of ammunition expended, M7+DL suffered fewer than thirty machine gun bullet strikes and was registered as sustaining less than 10 per cent damage to its airframe. Although this was the first incident involving enemy action, the first major loss occurred on 20 March 1940.

Ordered to operate off the Dutch coast, 3./806 had launched a patrol shortly after mid-day. At 4:30 hours, M7+EL (WNr 5164), with the crew of *Lt.z.S* Helmut Obermann (B), *Fw* Hermann Kasch (F), *Uffz* Robert Mehnert (Bm), and *ObFw* Alfred Hubrich (Bf), engaged fishing vessels, the AA defences of which damaged the aircraft's engines. In the engagement, both Obermann and Hubrich were wounded, while the damage necessitated a ditching off the Dutch coast, north-west of the Waddeneilanden, at 4:50 hours. Fortunately for the crew, soon after taking to their life raft they were rescued by the motor-cutter *Vier Gebroeders*. Landed at Ijmuiden the next day, the crew was repatriated to Germany as shipwrecked mariners. M7+EL was completely destroyed. The susceptibility of the Heinkel's engines to damage was further emphasised on 3 April when M7+CH (WNr 5094) was forced to ditch after an engine fire over the Kattegat. Having taken off at 8:30 hours from Holtenau on a routine reconnaissance operation, the crew experienced an engine fire, which forced them to ditch 3 km off the Hatter Rev, between the islands of Samsø and Sejrø. *Oblt.z.S* Adam Beck (B), *Fw* Heinrich Baasch (F), *Fw* Georg Juchelko (Bf), and *Uffz* Richard Bruhn (Bm) all escaped the stricken aircraft. Although fishing boats in the region came to the assistance, the crew refused any help. Drifting for several hours, the flyers finally came ashore near Lilleballe on the eastside of Samsø, where they were taken into custody by Danish police. Interned in the Flinchs Hotel in Tranebjergm, the crew was released on 9 April when the country was over-run by invading German forces.

The Junkers 88 and Redesignation

With the assault on Scandinavia came increased calls from Göring to reinforce his *Kampfgeschwader* by transferring control of maritime air units to the *Luftwaffe*. Likewise, the problems inherent with the He 111J had brought renewed calls for the *Gruppe* to re-equip with more reliable aircraft: three further technical incidents, two on 16 April and on one on 24 April, had beset the *Gruppe*'s Heinkels. Consequently, as April wore on into May plans were made to re-equip the *Gruppe* with the more reliable Ju 88. Commencing in June, all three *Staffeln* moved to Uetersen where they began replacing its Heinkels with the more reliable Junkers. By the end of June, the process was complete. In the meantime, discussions between Göring and Raeder meant the *Gruppe* was to be transferred for a brief period to the *Luftwaffe* before returning to naval control. However, the transfer in early July signalled the end of any maritime association, as the *Gruppe* was permanently redesignated *Kampfgruppe* 806. On 8 July, the unit was passed to the operational and administrative control of *Luftflotte* 3, and was destined to stay under *Luftwaffe* control until 1942, when its units were used to bolster *Kamfgeschwader* 54's operational efficiency.

12

Küstenfliegergruppe 906

Not a pre-war unit, *Küstenfliegergruppe* 906 was a product of the October 1939 reorganisation of naval air units. On 21 October 1939, *ObdL/Führungsstab* Order 5334/39 officially laid the foundations for the renumbering of all existing *Küstenfliegergruppen* (except *KüFlGr.* 106), and while it did create seemingly new units, vary little was new; *Stab* 906, 1, and 3 *Staffeln* had originally been the *Stab*, 1, and 3 *Staffeln* of *Küstenfliegergruppe* 706, while the 2 *Staffel* had been 2 *Staffel* of *Küstenfliegergruppe* 606. The wholesale change in unit designations meant little to the old units, whose personnel and equipment stayed, for the most part, largely unchanged.

Under the command of *Obstlt* Edart Hermann, the following comprised the *Stabsstaffel*: *Gruppe* Adjutant *Hptm* Bauer, *Offizer z.b.V Oblt.z.S* Boerricher, and *Technische Offizier Hptm* Holm. At the *Staffel* level, the various *Staffelkapitäne* included *Maj.* Kaiser of the 1 *Staffel, Hptm* Hans-Bruno von Laue of the 3 *Staffel*, and *Hptm* Kurt Stein of the 3 *Staffel*.

Sitzkrieg

Given the operational readiness of the *Gruppe*'s previous incarnations, operations were conducted along the lines already established. For the 1 *Staffel*, this usually meant coastal reconnaissance of the lower North Sea, Skagerrak, and Kattegat, while the 2 and 3 *Staffeln* occupied themselves with long-range reconnaissance of sea lanes and anti-submarine patrols over the mid North Sea and along the English respectively.

By November, the *Stab* and 1 *Staffel* had relocated to Pillau in East Prussia. However, contact with the enemy was rare; not until 7 November,

Staffel personnel of 3./906 gather in front of He 59 8L+RL during late 1939. As was the practice, the aircraft letter 'R' was painted in the *Staffel* colour of yellow.

when Do 18 (8L+BK) exchanged fire with Anson K6190, flown by Plt Off. Harper from 206 Squadron over the Hornum Sea, was the *Gruppe* blooded. At the time, the flying boat was so low over the water that Harper thought it had actually landed on the open sea. Armed with bombs, Plt Off. Harper tried bombing the Dornier, which inflicted only slight damage. Harper then turned and attacked the seaplane with his front guns, again inflicting minor damage. It was at this point in time that a second Do 18 appeared and came to the aide of 8L+BK. After a brief exchange of machine gun fire, Harper was forced to break off his attack and return to base with his ammunition expended.

Aside from reconnaissance and convoy patrol and escort duties, the 3 *Staffel* was assigned offensive operations. On the night of 21/22 November, the *Staffel* conducted the *Gruppe*'s first offensive mine-laying operation when three He 59s from Norderney dropped parachute aerial mines in the Thames Estuary and off Harwich. The following night, He 59s of 1 *Staffel*, in conjunction with other aircraft from 1 and 3 *Staffeln Küstenfliegergruppe* 106, conducted mine-laying sorties off the English coast.

These operations constituted the earliest mine-laying operations conducted by the *Luftwaffe*. Unfortunately for the Germans, the scale on which these operations were launched was limited, thereby restricting their success. Despite this, for the remainder of November and during the first week of December aerial mining was a regular feature of operations for the crews of 1 and 3./906. By December 1939, it was becoming obvious that the Heinkel 60 and 114s were no longer adequate for the operational requirements being placed on them. As a result, the 1 *Staffel* transferred from Pillau to Bug auf Rügen during the month to begin conversion training on the Heinkel 115.

Until this point, losses sustained by the *Gruppe* were negligible. However, over the winter of 1939-40 the technical inadequacies of the aircraft combined with unpredictable weather patterns in northern Europe presaged an increase in losses. Perhaps the strangest loss the *Gruppe* sustained occurred on 6 December, when Do 18 (W.Nr. 0811) 8L+FK from 2./906 was returning from a patrol and was engaged and fired at by a pilot from I./ZG 76 (possibly of the 2 *Staffel*). Having suffered 40 per cent damage, the pilot of the stricken Dornier was obliged to make an emergency landing, no doubt along with a few choice comments directed to the crew of the Bf 110 heavy fighter that had attempted to shoot them down. While there were no human losses, the incident served as a reminder of the constant need for vigilance while on operations.

Throughout December, the *Gruppe* continued to fly mine-laying sorties until losses sustained by the various *Küstenfliegerstaffeln* engaged

Mechanics reload the heavy armament on a Messerschmitt Bf 110 similar to that which intercepted 8L+FK on 6 December 1939.

Above and opposite: He 59 (Wnr 1848) of Seenotzentrale Boulogne – formerly of 3./906 – showing 20 per cent damage to the right rear stabilizer and lower right wing fabric. The damage is listed as having incurred on 2 August 1940 when the aircraft broke its moorings and drifted, hitting a breakwater. The scene is at Boulogne-sur-Mer. The aircraft *Stammkennzeichen* was NE+TA. The aircraft had previously served with 3./906 as 8L+UL.

in such work forced *Maj. Gen.* Köhler to call a temporary halt to such operations on the grounds that it was proving a heavy drain on personnel and equipment. Yet despite Köhler's ban, 906 carried out a few more aerial mining sorties until 17 December 1939, when all aerial mine-laying operations were stopped completely owing to the icing-up of the seaplane bases. Until this point, the *Gruppe* had participated in five dedicated mine-laying operations, which had altogether sewn forty-six LMA and twenty-two LMB mines.

Despite the worsening conditions and the icing-up of its seaplane bases, the *Gruppe* continued to carry on with operations whenever the opportunities presented themselves. At the same time, the losses continued to rise. By the close of 1939, ten weeks of operations had cost the *Gruppe* several wounded crewman and one killed in action. Four He 59 seaplanes had been lost or destroyed and another two had been damaged. Two Do 18s had been lost and another two damaged, and an He 114 was also lost.

Christmas and New Year had been a relatively quiet affair for the *Gruppe,* with operations curtailed due to weather, yet by the end of the first week in January the *Gruppe* was back in action and again suffering losses. Ironically, the first loss of 1940 was not a seaplane or flyboat, but a

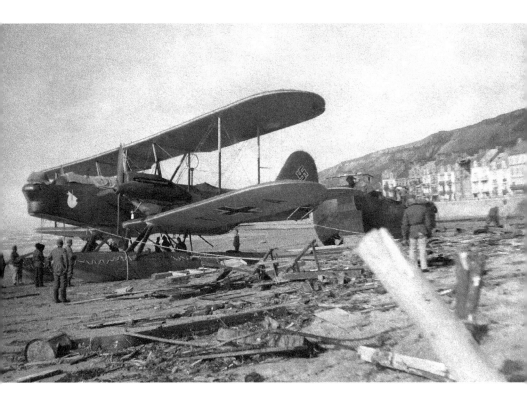

land-based bomber. On 5 January, a Heinkel 111J belonging to the 3./906 – undoubtedly used as a non-operational, general duties aircraft – suffered an engine failure, which necessitated a forced landing at Schwabisch Hall with 30 per cent damage. All those flying on board when the accident occurred landed safely, but the aircraft had a prolonged stay at Schwabisch Hall before returning to Norderney and its operating unit.

With the New Year also came a rotation in aircraft. From the 1 *Staffel*, three He 60s were transferred to Travemünde, and their places were taken by three similar aircraft from the 2./*Küstenfliegergruppe* 806, while a further two He 59s, accompanied by three crews, took off for Kiel-Holtenau. Not just aircraft needed servicing; establishments also needed supplementing. On 8 January, 3./906 noted that due to a lack of personnel, no operations for the day could be launched. With the winter sea ice forming, this did not seriously impact operational capabilities, but it did provide a unique portent for the fate of the *Gruppe* and *Küstenfliegergruppen* in general in later years.

During January, aircraft from 1 *Staffel* were distributed piecemeal around the German coastline. Having not yet transitioned to the He 115, the unit instead now operated He 60s and the aging He 59s. From 11 January, the *Staffel*'s aircraft were spread between Kiel (He 59), Bug (He 59), and Warnemünde (He 60). However, both Bug and Warnemünde were frozen over, so limited operations could be conducted from Kiel. In fact, from the middle of January to mid-March 1940 only 1./906 flew on operations, with both the 2 and 3 *Staffeln* being stood down for a period of rest, training, and re-equipping. Even still, during March 1 Staffel only managed 4,824 km, or 24 hours and 12 minutes flight time spread between seven aircraft.

The only notable exceptions to the sustained period off operations occurred on 12 January 1940 when *Lt.z.S* Steinhart, *Ufw* Schmidt, and *Uffz* Czech – all of 2 *Staffel* – were awarded the Iron Cross, Second Class, and on 19 January *Hptm* Werner Klümper was appointed as the new *Staffelkapitän* of 3 *Staffel*.

With no serious attempts at operations and few chances for non-operational flying, between the force landing at Schwabisch Hall of the He 111J on 5 January and 29 March 1940 the *Gruppe* suffered no serious losses. However, on 19 March six Do 18s of the 2./906 (aircraft letters A, E, G, H, M, and K) all suffered minor bomb-splinter damage during a Bomber Command raid on its base at Hörnum. The raid was specifically a reprisal. Two nights earlier, while attacking British shipping in Scapa Flow, German aircraft had dropped bombs over land, killing Mr James Isbister and wounding six others. Mr Isbister was the first civilian casualty suffered in Britain due to the actions of the enemy. In response, the British

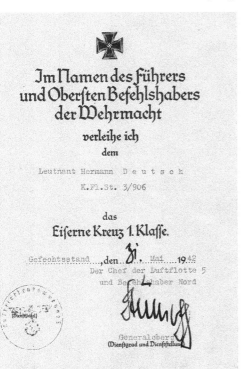

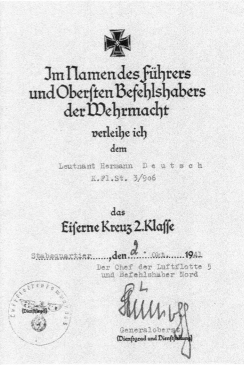

Award documents for *Leutnant* Hermann Deutsch of 3./906. Deutsch was promoted to *Oberleutnant* in 1943. (*Via S. Orchard*)

Government orders a reprisal raid on a seaplane base, but only where there were no civilians located nearby. On the night of 19/20 March, thirty Whitleys and twenty Hampdens were dispatched against Hörnum. 20 tons of HE and 1,200 incendiaries were dropped for the loss of one Whitley. Despite the effort, all the aircraft damaged were repaired within 48 hours.

Sometimes, the *Gruppe* was called upon to act as air sea rescue detachments. On 29 March 1940, three Ju 88s of II./KG 30 attacked the steam trawler Inverneil about 35-miles north-north-east of Buchan Ness. The attack, which lasted some 20 minutes, was eventually beaten off. In fact, even though the Inverneil had only a Lewis gun with which to defend itself, of the 300 rounds that were fired by the crew, sufficient enough damage was done to one of the Junkers that it later crashed into the sea at Cresswell Bay in Northumberland. Aboard the aircraft 4D+AP was the *Staffelkapitän* of 6./KG 30 Oberleutnant Quadt. The loss of the aircraft was reported and the following day, 2 *Staffel* detailed six aircraft to search for survivors. However, fierce snow-storms forced the abandonment of the operation with both EK and IK becoming lost. For the crew of 8L+GK (W.Nr. 0862), mechanical difficulties forced a ditching on the sea. Fortunately, cruising nearby was the U-boat U-30, which rescued the four stranded crew members, returning them to solid ground some days later. The Dornier, however, was left to drift and was not sighted again.

With the invasion of Norway in April 1940, all He 59 aircraft were withdrawn from service to equip a new transport unit. Taken at Stavanger, He 59 8L+SH can be seen wearing the vertical bars of II./KGzbV 108, over-painted on the old markings of 1./906.

Unternehmen Weserübung

During March 1940, the Germans made plans to invade Norway and Denmark. Given the logistical difficulties in operating against Norway, it was decided that a special transport *Gruppe* was to be raised consisting of seaplanes. The new *Gruppe – Kampfgruppe zur besonderen Verwendung* 108 – was to be equipped with the He 59 and Ju 52 seaplanes. Given the low numbers of these types, the new *Gruppe* sourced its aircraft from existing units. As a result, during late March and early April the Norderney based He 59s of the 3./906 were handed over to *KGzbV* 108 and the *Staffel* slowly converted to the He 115.

The change in aircraft did not hamper the 3./906 too greatly. On the afternoon of 9 April – *Wesertag* – elements of the *Staffel* undertook a reconnaissance operation to scout for the Royal Navy. For the most part, the *Gruppe*'s activities during the campaign in Norway consisted of maritime reconnaissance duties, although as the campaign came to a close in June anti-submarine patrols and convoy escort duties were increasingly added to the *Gruppe*'s responsibilities. Unfortunately, the low serviceability rates of the three flying *Staffeln* precluded daily operations, and in an effort to strengthen the *Gruppe*'s capacity to operate effectively, on 13 April the 5 *Staffel* of *Bordfliegergruppe* 196 came under the command of the *Stab./906*. With the capitulation of Norway in June 1940, the *Gruppe* once again focused its attentions on shipping in the North Sea and along the British east coast.

The Capture of HMS *Seal*

In 1940, the Royal Navy was heavily involved in the sowing of mines along the German coastline. Often, these operations were conducted by submarines. One such submarine was HMS *Seal*. On 29 April, the *Seal* set out from Immingham on the operation DF 7 with fifty mines. The operational aim was to lay a mine barrier near by the Swedish island Vinga, an area known to be frequented by German shipping heading to and from Norway. At 02:30 hours on 4 May, and close to the operational zone, the *Seal* was attacked by an He 115 from *Küstenfliegergruppe 706*. Sustaining no damage, Lonsdale was able to complete his operation. Lonsdale later noted that he had successfully laid the minefield at 09:00 hours on the morning of 4 May in about 45 minutes. However, at around 18:00 hours the *Seal* was heavily damaged by a mine that had been laid at a depth of 30 m. Surfacing the boat, Lonsdale realised that the crew's only chance was if they could reach Swedish territorial waters where they may be able to make repairs or await further help.

This page and opposite: Three views of the hapless HMS *Seal* after its capture by the Germans. The Porpoise class submarine later went on to be taken on strength by the *Kriegsmarine* as a U-boat in November 1940. The most important element of *Seal*'s capture was that it allowed the Germans to design a better firing pistol for torpedoes based upon the British designs.

Above and below: HMS *Seal* was not the only British submarine to fall fowl of air attack. On 5 July 1940, HMS *Shark* was crippled after being attacked by aircraft. Here are two poor quality photographs of the British submarine and her crew above deck after her surrender.

Unfortunately, the damage was so great that the *Seal* was only capable of making just a few knots on the surface. About an hour after the incident, the Ar 196s 6W+IN and 6W+EN of 5./ 196, flown by *Lt.z.S* Gunther Mehrens and *Lt.z.S* Karl-Ernst Schmidt respectively, spotted the British submarine. Mehrens attacked first with bombs and machine gun fire, followed by Schmidt. The attack injured several of the submarines crew and left Lonsdale with no choice but to surrender.

Seeing the submarine now dead in the water, Schmidt landed alongside while Mehrens returned to Aalborg to lead He 115 8L+CH, flown by *Lt.z.S* Nikolaus Broili of the 1./906, to the scene to complete the capture. Upon Broili's arrival, his observer swam across to the submarine to complete the capture and prevent any documents or useful intelligence from being destroyed. With the crew taken off later that day, the *Seal* was subsequently towed to Friederikshaven by UJ-22.

Operations in the West

Although operations in Norway were far from decided, on 10 May 1940 the German's launched their invasion of France. For the time being,

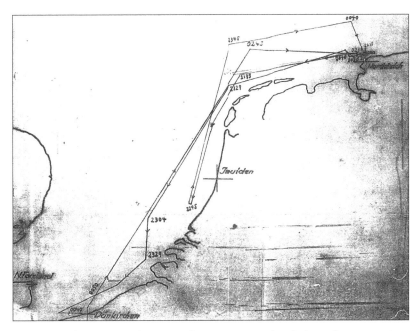

On 22 November 1939, elements of 3./906 were detailed to fly reconnaissance operations along the Dutch and French coastline. Flying out of Norderney this wartime document shows their operational flightpath.

the three flying *Staffeln* were located at Aalborg-See (1./906), Hörnum
(2./906), and Norderney (3./906). However, at the end of May 2./906 was
ordered to transfer to Stavanger-Sola See, where it arrived on 2 June. This
move was designed to push German naval air operations farther north,
as well as extending the range towards the North Atlantic by German air
forces. For the most part, during June the *Gruppe* participated little in
supporting operations against France and the British Expeditionary Force
there. Instead, it focused on convoy escort of shipping moving between
Germany, Sweden, and Denmark and the ongoing war against British
merchant shipping in the North Sea and along the British coast. To support
this, during July 1940 1./906 began transferring from Aalborg to Brest
Poulmic (Brest-South) in Brittany and Hourtin. The aim was to support
operations in conjunction with the four Do 18s of 2./106 based there
flying reconnaissance sorties to support the German U-boat campaign in
the Atlantic. At the same time, 2./906 was instructed to act as an air-sea
rescue unit in support of air operations against Britain, while at the end
of the month 3./906 transferred from Norderney to Schellingwoude in
Holland for operations under the direction of 9 *Fliegerdivison.*

    In September 1940, 2./906 began converting to the Blohm and Voss
Bv 138. Despite its promise, the new type proved a failure. It was found
that the hull, floats, and landing flaps all needed strengthening. It was
also found that the exhaust feed from the centre engine had a tendency
to become blocked, which resulted in a 70-hp loss in performance. As a
result, until early 1941 the *Staffel* only saw minimal service as the faults
were rectified.

1941: The Year of the Junkers

In October 1940, the Germans began preparing for the invasion of
Russia. By early 1941, German naval aircraft were based along the
western seaboard of Europe and Scandinavia, and while any operations
against Russia would not impact heavily on the *Küstenfliegergruppen*,
the move through the Baltic in the summer of 1941 saw elements of
Küstenfliegergruppe 506 and 906 exchange their naval aircraft for land-
based bombers.

    On 19 June 1941, 2./906 was ordered to begin converting to the Junkers
Ju 88. In order to carry this out, the unit moved from its base at Hörnum
See to Westerland. As conversion to the new type was completed, the crews
continued to operate against shipping off the east coast of the British Isles.
By this point in the war, British shipping defences were being increased. As
a result, *Küstenflieger* crews, although not barred from attacking shipping,

were instructed that attacks were forbidden if there was insufficient cloud cover, ships were flying balloons or were supported by strong defences, or if there was too much daylight for a surprise attack. In such cases, crews were to seek alternative targets on land.

Operation Beowulf II and a Redesignation

On 21 September 1941, four Ju 88s left Westerland as an advance party of 2./906 for Riga in Latvia to serve under *Fliegerführer Ostsee* (the tactical designation of the *Stab./906* until mid-1941). While the rest of the *Staffel* transferred several days later, the vanguard commenced operations against Soviet airfields and other targets on Saaremaa (Ösel) off the Estonian west coast. These operations were designed to support the German amphibious operations against the islands, which were quickly captured.

While 2./906 was conducting these operations, orders were received on 27 September that stated from 6 October 1941, 2./906 would be renumbered as 2./506 and vice versa. This meant that 2./906 would relinquish its Ju 88s and return to maritime operations with the He 115 flying out of Brest-Süd, while 2./506 would become a complete land-based unit, changing its designation from *Küstenfliegergruppe* to *Kampfgruppe*. The change of designation also saw 2./906 now fall under the direction of *Stab./406*, which was involved in supporting U–boat operations over the Bay of Biscay and anti-shipping sorties over the Bristol and southern exit to the English Channels. Although 1941 had witnessed an increase in British defences, the *Gruppe* saw out the year having suffered only thirty losses to all causes, an increase of just three from the twenty-seven lost in 1940.

1942 and the Convoy Battles

By 1942, the *Gruppe*'s various *Staffeln* were all again based in the west – 1./906 under *Hptm* Otto-Friedrich Werner at Brest-Hourtin, 2./906 under *Hptm* Siegfried Kriebel at Brest-Süd, and 3./906 under *Oblt* Wolf-Friedrich Schöne at Tromsø. Yet the *Gruppe*'s successes were soon to be reversed.

The growing need for aircraft to operate against land-based targets and Göring's dominance of the *Luftwaffe* meant the anti-shipping and U-boat support roles were becoming increasingly marginalised. In the second week of April, both the *Stab* and 2 *Staffel* were ordered disbanded; the seven crews and eight He 115s of the latter were parcelled out to 1./406 and 1./906. Both these units were in need of reinforcing, as throughout

Escort duty for capital ships was a rarity, although it was no less hazardous than any other type of operation. On 12 April 1940 He 115 8L+GL (WNr 2401) crashed whilst making a steep turn patrolling over the cruiser *Lützow. Lt.z.S* Wolfgang Reich (B) was killed in the accident while *Uffz* Nikolaus May (F) and *Gfr* Gunther Konnick (Bf) were both injured. (*Via D. Wadman*)

the winter of 1941-42 the British and Americans had been increasing the number and size of Lend Lease convoys headed for Russia. On 2 April, 1./906, now based at Stavanger, had succeeded in sinking the tanker *Rigmor* (6305 GRT), but the more notable success for the *Gruppe* occurred on 4 July.

The Russia-bound PQ17 had left Reykjavik on 27 June. During the morning, the *Staffelkapitän* of 1./906, *Hptm* Peuckert, had led a formation of seven He 115s on attack against the ships of PQ 17. Although the weather was atrocious, Peuckert was able to find the convoy in the Barents Sea, about 35-miles north-east of Bear Island in position 75°49′ N 22°15′ E, and immediately order an attack. Flying low over the water, Peuckert released a single torpedo that struck the American freighter *Christopher Newport* (7200GRT), which was carrying 8,200 tons of war material

Long-range operations with the diesel-powered Bv 138 sometimes allowed for mid-Atlantic refuelling stops from patrolling U-boats. Obviously such operations were risky and needed the calmest weather to be completed. (*Via D. Wadman*)

amidships. As Rolph Pohler, a crew mate on board Peuckert's aircraft, later recalled, 'We were flying a wide search partly above the clouds and partly through the fog near the water surface when our captain suddenly hit upon the convoy. We attacked immediately and launched a torpedo, hitting one vessel.'

The torpedo tore a large hole in the starboard side of the hull and flooded the engine room, killing an officer and two men, as well as destroying the steering gear. Unable to steer, the crew abandoned ship. At 08:08 hours, U-457 fired a single torpedo at the *Christopher Newport*, which sent her to the bottom.

Operations against the Arctic convoys were often conducted under difficult conditions. The winter ice cap in the Arctic Ocean that forced the convoys to sail close to the Norwegian coastline also brought with it few hours of daylight and temperamental weather patterns. Although Peuckert's success was fortuitous, it was short lived. The increasing protection that the Arctic convoys received greatly impacted the ability of 1 and 3./906 (now both based in Norway) to influence the trade war. The final PQ convoy to be attacked by the *Gruppe* brought no success, but lost He 115 8L+FH (WNr 2247) and all her crew.

Although the *Gruppe*'s two remaining *Staffeln* continued to operate against shipping in northern waters, they did so at increasingly lengthening odds. As the war in Russia shifted focus towards the southern sector and the fight for Stalingrad and the Caucasus oil fields, *Luftflotte* 5 was increasingly denuded of aircraft to support operations elsewhere. The slow and lumbering He 115s proved no match for ships anti-aircraft fire, while the introduction of CAM ships and escort carriers into the theatre virtually precluded the *Küstenfliegerstaffeln* from any form of offensive operations.

The Loss of 8L+IH

Given the sparsely populated region of Northern Norway, Finland, and Russia, and the rugged terrain, seaplanes were often used to fly in and out supplies and long-range reconnaissance or special operations teams. For the most part, these operations were conducted by the *Versuche Verbande, Oberbefehlshaber der Luftwaffe,* or *Kampfgeschwader* 200. However, sometimes these operations were conducted by ordinary units and crews on secondment to the aforementioned *Gruppen*. On 22 October 1942, the crew of *Fw* August Archer (F), *Oblt* Kurt Helf (B), *Uffz* Ernst Leuenhagen (Bf), and *Uffz* Stefan Kuballa (Bs) were detailed to fly an operation on behalf of the 2./*Vers.Verb.Ob.d.L.* in support of a long-range Estonian volunteer unit deep behind Russian lines.

The ill-fated 8L+CH is prepared for an operation. (*Via D. Wadman*)

The plan called for the German crew to stage through Santahamina, 6.5-km south-east of Helsinki, from where they would then fly to Lake Jungozero in the Lake Onega area. Unbeknownst to the Germans, the thirteen Estonians had been captured by the NKVD.[5] Under duress, the Estonians had requested an extraction by the *Luftwaffe* at a time and place of the NKVD's choosing. Quite what happened next is opened to conjecture, but after landing, the German crew was captured, and along with the Estonians, executed by the Russians. Although this was the *Gruppe*'s only recorded loss for a three month period, it underscored the increasingly difficult odds that the *Küstenfliegergruppen* were operating against.

1943: The End

With the increasingly potent convoy escorts posing a problem for anti-shipping operations in the Arctic, the *Gruppe* found an increasing amount of work acting as convoy escorts for German shipping in Norwegian waters and fjords. On New Year's Day 1943, the *Gruppe*'s strength stood at seven He 115LTs of the 1./906 and nine Bv 138Cs of the 3./906.

With the air war intensifying over Germany and operations in Russia against land-based objective becoming more and more of a priority, the

Küstenfliegergruppen's role in aerial operations shrank dramatically. The *Luftwaffe*'s creation and expansion of its own naval air units likewise hampered the efforts of the *Küstenfliegergruppen*, and by mid-1943 few of the original *Staffeln* created in the lead up to and early months of the war still existed. In July 1943, 3./906 was disbanded and renamed as the 2 *Staffel* of the *Luftwaffe*'s own *Seeaufklärungsgruppe* 131, while in February of 1943 the last remaining *Staffel* of the *Gruppe* 1./906 had begun a slow conversion to land-based aircraft.

Originally, it had been intended that 1./906 would convert to the Heinkel He 111. On 10 September, the conversion from maritime aircraft to land-based bombers was complete, and although by now the *Staffel* had retrained on the Ju 88, the outcome was the same. On that day, the *Staffel* was effectively disbanded when it was redesignated as the 8 *Staffel* of *Kampfgeschwader* 26.

Throughout its nearly three years of service, the *Gruppe* had suffered ninety-nine flying personnel losses to all causes, including those limited to injuries sustained in combat by returning aircraft and those aircraft damaged in storms while at the moorings. Although the unit was one of the more obscure *Küstenfliegergruppen*, it had served with distinction for almost its entire career in the western and northern theatres of operation. It had been responsible for sinking or damaging almost 100,000 tons of shipping and could claim to be the instigator of the German aerial mining campaign against British shipping in 1939. Although survived by a handful of other *Küstenfliegerstaffeln*, the *Gruppe*'s fate was soon shared by them as the war in the air moved increasingly away from operations against shipping and Göring tightened his control of all air units in Germany.

13
AS/88

By mid-1930, Spain was a country divided. The conservative, Catholic Nationalists arguing for a return to the monarchy were increasingly opposed by a coalition of forces that held a majority in the Spanish parliament. Amid this turmoil rose a right-wing Fascist party known as the Falange. Its leader, Calvo Sotelo, was arrested and later assassinated by Government forces on 13 July 1936. Sotelo's murder thus became the catalyst for all-out civil war. On 17 July 1936, General Francisco Franco and other military and political leaders went into open revolt, the most successful of which was their seizure of Morocco. However, Madrid and Barcelona remained loyal to the Government. There followed a series of confused battles between Nationalist and what later became known as Republican forces. Meanwhile in Morocco, General Franco had arrived to take charge of the well-equipped garrison there. The difficulty for Franco and the Nationalist cause was that much of the Spanish Air Force and Navy had allied itself to the Government and thus offered no help in transferring Nationalist forces to the mainland. Recognising an opportunity to expand the influence of Germany in Europe, Hitler agreed to provide military support for Franco's cause. By 31 July, German aircraft and personnel were on their way to Spanish Morocco. This expeditionary force later became known as the Condor Legion.

While much of the force sent to aide Franco were land-orientated, a small group of naval aviators were supplied, not just as air escorts for German and Nationalist shipping travelling to and from the region, but to act as air-sea reconnaissance and anti-shipping forces. The first of this naval air detachment arrived on 18 September 1936 when the German steamer *Wigbert* ferried a lone He 59 and He 60 to Spain. This was followed by the arrival of two further He 60s crated aboard the passenger vessel *Esenach*

A stern view of the pocket battleship *Admiral Graf Spee* as the German naval representative at the May 1937 Spithead review at the time of the coronation of His Majesty King George VI. Clearly visible on the catapult abaft the funnel is one of her two embarked He 60D aircraft. They were later replaced by a pair of Arado Ar 196 floatplanes shortly before she sailed for the South Atlantic in August 1939. They made five patrols off Spain during the war: 20 August – 9 September 1939, 13 December 1936 – 14 February 1937, 2 March – 6 May 1937, 23 June – 7 August 1937 and 7-18 February 1938. (*Via D. Wadman*)

at Seville on 14 October. Accompanying these aircraft were *Hptm* Karl-Heinz Wolff (*Beobachter*), *Lt* Siegmund Storp (*Flugzeugführer*), and two mechanics. Immediately, work started on assembling the aircraft, which was completed in record time at the Construcciones Aeronáuticas Sociedad Anónima (C.A.S.A) at Cádiz. The following day, the He 59 was used to bomb the aerodrome at El Rompedizo. While humble, this beginning signalled the German intention of actively participating in the intervention of Spanish loyalist forces. With the civil unrest deepening, the He 60s based at Cádiz began flight patrols along the Mediterranean coastline. However, on 6 November the battle cruiser *Admiral Scheer* was diverted to recover a He 60 after a forced landing during a reconnaissance sortie. This, and a further ditching (and subsequent recovery by the cruiser *Königsberg* on 19 December) of an He 59 that force landed at sea, provided early signs of weakness in German naval air technology and equipment.

On 27 November, the German merchant vessel the *Stassfurt* landed two more He 59 seaplanes in Spain. Accompanying these airframes were the observers *Oblt* Werner Klümper and *Lt* Dieter Leicht, and two pilots, *OFw* Johann Gaesslere and *Uffz* Bernhardt Winse. At the same time, at the end of November the Condor Legion was officially formed, and the seaplane unit based in Spain henceforth became known as *Aufklärungsstaffel See /88*, or AS/88 for short. Throughout the conflict, Germany sent a total of seventeen He 59s to Spain, at a cost of RM 312,290 each, and eight He 60s. Meanwhile, a third transport of aircraft had been arranged, and on 23 December a further two He 60s were landed by the German vessel *Capri*.

Over the Christmas period, the seaplanes and their crews were moved from Cádiz to Melilla in North Africa. While the facilities there were inferior to those at Cádiz, the relocation afforded better tactical deployment by the unit. At the same time, AS/88 received orders to begin experimenting with the Norwegian Horten torpedoes that had been sent from Germany. The orders were to test the entry behaviour, running characteristics, and effect on targets when they presented themselves. It was not long before such an occasion presented itself.

A New Year and the First Successful Interceptions

On 30 January 1937, a He 60 piloted by *Lt* Dieter Leicht spotted a loaded steamer sailing just off the south coast of Spain between Almeria and Malaga. When news was received at Melilla, a He 59 was fitted with a torpedo and ordered to engage. The observer aboard was *Oblt* Werner Klümper, who later recorded:

The weather was good and the freighter was easily spotted. I made a textbook approach, released the torpedo, and turned away. At the same instant, my flight engineer informed me that the torpedo had not dropped. There was no indication of anything wrong on the release panel; all the control lights were properly lit. We would repeat the attack. I turned the aircraft around and made a new approach. Once again the torpedo failed to release.

An electrical fault with the release mechanism meant it was not until a third approach that the flight engineer was able to release the torpedo. However, as would often prove the case in the following years, the torpedo failed to run true, instead running a circular pattern. However, Klümper's attack was the first air-dropped torpedo operation against shipping since the end of the First World War. Undeterred, Klümper returned to Melilla where he took off again in a second He 59, this time armed with two 250-kg bombs. Relocating the vessel, Klümper:

> Released the bombs from 1,000 m, but once again things did not go as planned. I had selected train release but both bombs fell at the same time. But one has to be lucky sometimes, both bombs struck amidships – direct hit! There was a tremendous explosion, then we had to turn away as three enemy fighters were coming toward us from the mainland. Before we lost sight of it we saw the freighter turning towards the coast.

Unbeknownst to Klümper and his crew at the time, the vessel was the 1,253-ton Spanish mail ship *Delfin*, which belonged to the Transmediterranean Company and was acting as a mail carrier in the Republican zone. While the Republicans later claimed the vessel was lost as a result of combined submarine and air action, its interception and subsequent loss, albeit under trying circumstances, proved naval-air anti-shipping forces were capable

The mainstay of operations in Spain was the He 59. Standardised camouflage is applied to the aircraft.

of intercepting and destroying enemy vessels underway at sea.

The following day, Klümper was again airborne, this time accompanied by the He 60 of *Lt* Leicht. Word had reached AS/88 that a Republican vessel had left Orán with 200 Spanish volunteers for the Republican cause. At about 11:00 hours local time, the two German aircraft spotted what was later identified as the 2,733-ton *Nuria Ramos*, under the command of Captain Estrader, underway near Cabo de Palos. Unwilling to attack a vessel with so many people aboard, Klümper decided to employ a *ruse de guerre* to lure the ship into safe harbour where it could be captured. Taking up station to one side of the vessel, Klümper watched as the He 60 flew low over the steamer from astern and dropped a message pouch onto the deck. Written in Spanish, the message read, 'Halt immediately – no radio communications or you will be torpedoed. Further orders will follow.' At the same time, the He 60 crew dropped several light bombs fitted with impact fuses into the water in front of the ship. Shortly afterwards, a second message was dropped: 'Go to maximum speed, course south. If you deviate from this order you will be torpedoed at once.' Klümper continued to circle close to the freighter so that the torpedo could be seen and the ship picked up speed and turned onto a southerly course. It was at this point that Leicht was forced to turn for home, low on fuel, leaving Klümper in a precarious position. Similarly low on fuel, Klümper transmitted to Estrader that he would be escorted on the new course by a submerged

Supporting the He 59 was the smaller He 60. Here, standardised markings are applied to this aircraft.

submarine that had orders to sink the vessel if it attempted to make a run for a Republican port. With little else left to do, Klümper then turned for home.

The following day, 1 February, Klümper was out at dawn, searching for the Spanish vessel. To his surprise, he found her obediently holding course, slightly displaced by a storm during the night. The vessel entered Melilla as the first prize vessel of the war.

The First Loss

The success enjoyed by AS/88, and Klümper in particular, was soon over-shadowed by the loss of Dieter Leicht. On 5 February, Leicht had been detailed to bomb troop concentrations as part of a Nationalist offensive to capture Málaga. Intercepted by the I-15 of Charle Koch, Leicht's He 59, coded 523, crashed into the sea. Severely injured, Leicht was dragged from the wreck by his crew mates, who were later rescued by the Nationalist cruiser *Canarias*. Yet nothing could be done and Leicht later died of wounds. Compounding the loss, as 523 went down it collided with and damaged the port wing of He 60, coded 512 and christened *Sea Beast*, which was forced to make an emergency landing on the sea nearby, where it and its crew were later recovered by the *Canarias*.

Changes All Round

By mid-February, AS/88 found itself transferred to Málaga, an even more primitive operating base than Melilla. At the same time, *Staffelkapitän* Wolff was recalled to Berlin and was replaced by *Hptm* Gunther Klünder. This quick rotation reflected the German High Command's desire to expose as many personnel to combat conditions as possible. By way of reinforcement, two additional He 59 and He 60 aircraft are sent to the unit.

Throughout February, the pace and style of operations remained constant. Reconnaissance of sea-lanes and the bombing of coastal targets remained the primary focus of AS/88. Then in April, the Staffel began the drawn-out process of transferring to Cádiz, which was completed by 18 April. Three days later, on 21 April, He 60 513 *Sea Wolf* crashed on takeoff, injuring the Spanish pilot Maj. Rosi (Spanish) and injuring the German observer whose name was only reported as Mahi. Requiring extensive repairs, it would be some time before the *Sea Wolf* was again operational. Somewhat offsetting this loss, on 25 April the *Staffel* received a Ju 52/3m (W) aircraft that was henceforth employed in liaison and transport duties.

Sometimes the markings scheme varied a little. Here a torpedo-equipped He 59 sports a death's head emblem superimposed on the nose of the aircraft.

The trickle of replacement crews and parts put a heavy strain on operations. While *Lt.z.S* Ernst-Heinrich Thomsen departed 3./ *Küstenfliegergruppe* 106 on 15 June 1937 as a replacement observer for AS/88, it was not until 7 July that three badly needed BMW VI U engines were delivered as spares for the He 59s. Despite this, morale remained high. On 28 June, the He 59 coded 522 had encountered a Republican Dornier Wal flying boat on patrol north-east of Cabo de Palos. In the lumbering dogfight that ensued, the Republican aircraft was shot down. Aboard were Lt Jaime Fernández Villalba (pilot), Lt Gonzalo Rodriguez Hernández (radio operator), Lt Luis Sarabia Hurtado (flight engineer and bombardier – KIA) and Corporal Machinegunner-Bombardier Francisco Caballero Sandoval (gunner – WIA), who were later rescued by the British steamship *Nailsea*.

Blockading the Mediterranean

On 17 July 1937, the commander of the Nationalist blockade authorised attacks on all Spanish harbours, as long as there were no British ships at anchor or blockade runners flying the Greek, Panamanian, Danish, or Norwegian flags. Part of this meant the seaplanes of AS/88 were to operate in close liaison with Spanish authorities in observing the enemy fleet, undertaking aggressive action against any located enemy forces both at sea and in port, bombing missions against coastal military targets, and attacking Republican shipping in territorial waters or any ship attempting to break the blockade. Coinciding with this, the *Staffel* received its third commander since its arrival in Spain the previous September. At the end of July, *Hptm* Klünder was replaced by *Maj.* Hans Hefele, formerly the *Staffelkapitän* of 3./*Küstenfliegergruppe* 206.

Hefele's introduction to operational activities was immediate. On 30 July 1937, a patrol by three He 59s spotted a Republican convoy off Arenys de Mar, consisting of the Greek merchant *Laris* (camouflaged as the Panamanian vessel *Chepo*) the destroyers *Almirante Valdes* and *Escano*, and torpedo boats 31 and 41. Engaging, the torpedo-equipped seaplanes hit the *Laris* in the stern, killing four and forcing it to run aground near Calella, while the *Almirante Valdes* was damaged in the bows and the torpedo boat 41 was claimed as sunk. To supplement these achievements, a

In order to attack enemy concentrations or shipping, the He 59 was equipped with a 20-mm cannon in the forward observer's position. Even in defence, the weapon proved effective.

Republican Breguet XIX was also claimed as shot down. However, during the operation Hefele's He 59 was forced down by enemy fire south of Blanes. In a familiar operation, it was the Nationalist cruiser *Canarias* that came to the rescue, retrieving Hefele and his crew and taking the damaged He 59 under tow. They arrived in Pollensa the following day.

This success was followed up in August with the bombing of Barcelona on the night of 3/4, during which further damage was inflicted to the Greek ship *Laros*. The following week, on 12 August, *Lt.z.S* Hans Reefe (B), *Uffz* Peter Eberhard (F), *Uffz* Mauderer (Bm), and *Uffz* Heinrich Schindler (h.B) intercepted and attacked the Danish refrigerator ship *Edith* (1,566 tons) 40 miles off Tortosa. Backing this up, a fortnight later, He 59s 528 and 529 successfully intercepted the British ship *Noemijulia* (2,499 tons), underway near Barcelona. While these aircraft were intercepted by a flight of two Republican fighters, no damage was inflicted.

While the interception of shipping and the bombing of coastal targets continued, it became increasingly clear that Republican defensive measures were improving. At the end of September, *Lt.z.S* Thomsen was forced down over the sea between Barcelona and Pollensa by an I-16, while further damage to another He 59 was inflicted on 3 December by I-15s during an attack on rail installations at Benicarlo. Although these incidents did not incur any losses, on 23 December He 59, coded 531, was lost after it was attacked by several Republican fighters. The unit had sent two He 59s on a coastal bombing operation when the incident occurred. Forced down with major damage, the crew of 531 manage to land 2 km offshore, where they were rescued by the second aircraft. He 59 531 was left ablaze on the sea and later sank.

1938

Throughout 1937, AS/88 had slowly handed over its He 60s to the Spaniards to operate independently. The removal of the smaller coastal patrol aircraft signalled a more intensive role for the Germans operating in Spain. The departure of the He 60s was also accompanied during January 1938 by the replacement of *Hptm* Hefele as *Staffelkapitän*, who returned to Germany, by *Hptm* Martin Harlinghausen. An experienced officer and previous *Staffelkapitän* of 3./506, Harlinghausen inherited a unit that was greatly experienced. Despite this, Harlinghausen did not have long before he had to confront the realities of war. On 13 January, *Uffz* Harald Kahl (Bm) was killed when the He 59 he was flying in crashed during bad weather. On 15 January, his coffin was sent to Cádiz, from where it was to be repatriated to Germany.

Harlinghausen's arrival brought with it a change in tactics. As the He 59 had a low cruising speed, it was possible to detect the aircraft before it commenced an attack. To combat this, Harlinghausen began experimenting with a new attack method. On 19 January, he took off at 05:00 hours local time as an observer with *Lt* Zenker (F), Hinterberger (Bf), and Schmehl (Bm) for an attack on harbour installations at Valenica. Approaching the target area, Harlinghausen ordered Zenker to reduce the engine speed to idle. Loosing speed, the aircraft descended from 3,500 m to 50 m. Harlinghausen released his bombs over the extensive fuel dump, the *Campsa*, having gained complete surprise. With the release of the bombs, Zenker applied full throttle and claimed away from the target area as the gunners aboard the aircraft strafed searchlight and flak batteries in the area. So successful was this new method in bombing that it became the preferred tactic for the remainder of AS/88's time in Spain. However, while the run-in to the target was masked, the aircraft still remained vulnerable during the climb away from the target at low altitude, a point brought home during March when the unit lost two aircraft to AA fire.

On 15 March, He 59 529 received damage from 20-mm anti-aircraft fire mounted on a train near Vinaroz. With little option, pilot *Ofw* Alfred Tonollo was forced to crash land his aircraft nearby. While the crew, which consisted of *Ofw* Rudolf Rücker, *Ofw* Hermann Strohmaier (B),

During the conflict the aircraft of the unit adopted different motifs. Here a He 59 and He 60 of the unit sport the ace of spades on the nose, while in the background is the tail section of an Italian Cant Z501 flying boat.

Ofw Bruno Stötzer, and *Alferez Piloto* Jose Caetano Rocha Sepulveda Velloso, a Portuguese volunteer who was temporarily assigned to the unit, were able to set the aircraft alight, they were soon captured by Republican forces. They were later exchanged and returned to the *Staffel*. This loss was compounded on 21 March when *Oblt* Hajo Jürgens (B), *Lt* Karl Zunker (F), *Uffz* Kurt Keitzel (Bf), and *Uffz* Kurt Werner (Bm) were killed after they were intercepted by Jose Sarrio Calatayud of no. 71 mixed Group. Jürgens and his crew had been detailed to bomb the railway bridge and station at Tortosa. At low altitude, around 05:00 hours the He 59 was intercepted and set alight. Three members of the crew were burned to death, while a fourth was later rescued severely injured, but died as a result of his wounds.

The ill-fated attack on Tortosa represented a renewed effort by the *Staffel* to intercept and disrupt enemy troop transports in the region. Increasingly, the He 59s focused on rail installations. During the last week of March and into the first half of April, the primary focus was the Bernicarlo rail junction, its station, and turntable. By now, the *Staffel* relied upon the He 59 almost exclusively, having handed over all but one of its He 60s to the Spanish. On 26 April, AS/88 was officially requested to support the Legion's bomber unit K/88 in bombing coastal facilities that were opposing Nationalist ground forces in their drive to Valencia.

On 21 June 1938, the unit scored only its second successful torpedo operation when the British merchant vessel *Thorpeness*, (4,800 tons) was torpedoed. The *Staffel* later reported that the He 59 coded 530, captained by *Hptm* Harlinghausen, had successfully torpedoed a vessel in the midships after a run of 1 minute and 35 seconds. While the *Staffel* would sink forty-seven ships and capture one other, totalling almost 90,000 tons during the cause of the war, the introduction of the aerial torpedo did not significantly improve the lethality of the unit's war against shipping. Limited and sometimes faulty supplies, combined with the difficulties inherent in such operations, meant AS/88's success rate was negligible. Despite this, Martin Harlinghausen was so enthusiastic that during the Second World War he developed the theory leading to the formation of an entire *Gruppe* of *Kampfgeschwader* 26 being employed only in torpedo operations.

By the end of autumn 1938, Nationalist victories were mounting. However, there was still determined resistance put up against operations by AS/88. On 2 August, while undertaking a harassing attack against industrial targets in Paitrosos, an He 59 was damaged and forced to make an emergency landing on the sea near Vinaroz. A coastal trawler rescued the crew, who were unhurt except for the pilot *Uffz* Euen (F), who sustained minor injuries. On 29 August, He 59 532 was destroyed in an accident, while on 2 November a further He 59 was lost when it was shot down near Santa Cristina de Aro. These losses, while intermittent, were worrying, and they highlighted the vulnerability of the Heinkel seaplanes, a conclusion emphasised by the loss of *Lt* Schmidt and his crew on 31 December when they were lost after being intercepted by Republican Fighters over Vils, near Blanes. Despite this, operations continued as it became increasingly clear that the Nationalist forces were beginning to overwhelm Republican forces.

1939

Throughout January 1939, AS/88 focused on traffic and troop movements around the Malgrat region. Aside from an attempted intercept by three Republican fighters on 28 January, very little enemy air activity was noted for the month. However, by the end of January targets again focused more on ports and coastal shipping. On the night of 30 January, two He 59s patrolled the waters around Cap de Creus, while on the night of 2 February, harbour installations at San Feliu de Guixols were attacked, and over a period of the two nights, 8-10 February, approximately 15 tons of

Sporting the Ace of Spades emblem, this He 60 is prepared to be winched into the water in readiness for another operational flight.

high explosives were dropped on the port of Rosas and Puerto de la Selva, as well as shipping in the waters around Cape Creus.

The improved pace of operations meant that on 12 February AS/88 could only report seven serviceable He 59s and one He 60 at Pollensa. This number was further eroded the following day when a lone He 59 with no fighter escort was shot down by three Republican fighters. The dwindling number of aircraft proved a dire warning for the future of naval aviation in Germany in the years to come. Hampered by a lack of crews, aircraft, supplies, and equipment, the unit found it difficult to launch sustained and heavy attacks on enemy forces. The situation was not helped with the loss of a further two He 59s – one shot down by Republican Fighters near Cartagena on 5 February and a second destroyed in an accident on 22 of the same month.

The End

During March 1939, Martin Harlinghousen was replaced as *Staffelkapitän* by *Hptm* Helmer Smidt. This change in command also heralded the arrival of two of the new Heinkel seaplane prototype He 115s on 26 March. Wearing the registrations D-AOHS and D-ANPT, and flown by *Leutnante* Fiehn, Jandrey, and Wachsmuh, the aircraft land at Puerto Pollenso. The aircraft had been sent for testing under operation conditions, but the collapse of the Republican forces meant they saw no action. With no testing under combat conditions, both aircraft were eventually sent back to Travemünde. For the remainder of the conflict, AS/88 continued to fly patrols. Finally, on 26 May 1939 the last of the unit's personnel left Spain and the Condor Legion was officially disbanded. Throughout the conflict, some 355 personnel had been associated with the unit, 17 of whom became casualties. For many of the personnel that returned to Germany, the combat experience they gained in Spain helped guide the development of operations undertaken by the respective *Küstenfliegergruppen* to which they were assigned. Unfortunately for these men and their future comrades, the lessons of what a well-supplied and large force of naval aviation forces could achieve was wasted on a German High Command that focused its attentions on Continental ambitions.

14

Sonderstaffeln

Very little is known about the unit. Formed as a coastal patrol unit on 12 February 1942, it was comprised mostly of Estonian volunteers. Originally, the Estonian airmen had been administratively transferred to the Red Army during the Soviet occupation in 1940. However, when war between Germany and Russia broke out most of the airmen succeeded in escaping from the Jägala Training Camp and fleeing to the Germans. Having avoided being dragooned into Soviet service, Gerhard Buschmann, an ethnic German of Tallin, began setting up an aviation unit to aide the Germans.

An Abwehr officer, *Oblt* Buschmann's volunteer unit was supplied with captured military aircraft, including Ar 95 seaplanes, at least two ex-Polish RWD-8s, four ex-Estonian PTO-4, and four Stampe et Vertongen SV 5 aircraft, as well as a Miles Magister and Dragon Rapide. At its peak, the unit also operated thirty-four He-50 and thirteen Fokker C-VEs, and possibly some He 60s. Although not recognised by the *Luftwaffe*, the unit adopted SB+A? as its unofficial *verbandskennzeichen*. Known aircraft markings of the unit include SB+AA, SB+AB, SB+AC, SB+AD (PTO-4s), SB+AF (Miles Magister), SB+AH (Dragon Rapide), and SB+AJ (RWD-8).

Initially, the unit reported to the commander of the SS and police in Estiona. However, during December 1942 Heinrich Himmler took control of the *Sonderstaffel*. The unit's first combat patrol was on 11 March 1942 by a PTO-4 aircraft in the Gulf of Finland; reconnaissance of this area was the main tactical focus of the *Staffel* until April 1943, when the *Luftwaffe* absorbed the unit and used its personnel, now numbering some 200-odd men, to form the basis of the 1 *Staffel* of *Aufklärungsgruppe* 127.

A PTO-4 of *Sonderstaffel* Buschmann. The unit was not allocated its own *Verbandkennzeichen*, so instead adopted the unofficial SB+?? on its aircraft. (*Via D. Wadman*)

Küstenstaffel Krim

As the German Army began a slow process of retreat in Russia, it became obvious that reconnaissance of Soviet shipping in the Black Sea and along the Crimean coast was necessary. As a result, during August 1943 *Küstenstaffel Krim* was raised to operate in close conjunction with the 3 *Staffel* of *Fernaufklärungsgruppe* 11. Nominally placed under the command of IV *Fliegerkorps*, the unit acted autonomously in its reconnaissance operations.

Despite official designation in 1943, there had been a reconnaissance presence in the Crimea since 1942, when on 30 July *Oblt* Hans Klimmer had been placed in command of a reconnaissance unit, the function of which was to provide meteorological and shipping reconnaissance in the region. Due to shortages of production and the expanded needs of the *Luftwaffe*, the unit was provided with twenty-four obsolescent Focke Wulf Fw 58 'Weihe' aircraft, commandeered from *Kampffliegerschule* 1, based in Tutow. Of the twenty-four commandeered, the factory codes of all but six are known. The aircraft taken were as follows: BB+GI, BO+MD, CA+WU, CP+HW, CW+HP, DA+FX, DK+BA, DK+MB, GC+AZ, NV+KB, PI+NK, PW+AO, RC+NX, RD+NJ, RG+NX, TX+HM, VB+BW, XP+HW, XW+HP.

Although the Fw 58 only had a range of 676 km (420 miles), it was intended any long-range reconnaissance required of the region would be conducted by the 4 *Staffel* of *Fernaufklürungsgruppe* 122, then based at Kertsh. Between August 1942 and October 1943, the unit operated out of Bagerowo on the Kerch Peninsula and flew almost daily sorties.

From June to August 1943, the Fw 58 was slowly withdrawn from service and replaced by Bf 110 heavy fighters. By September, the unit had on strength eleven Bf 110s of various versions. Some of these aircraft had come direct from the factory and still retained their factory codes, which included the following: CC+MX, CE+CB, DE+YK, DH+EO, NH+EO, TE+SG, VE+VL, VE+VS. At the same time the unit began re-equipping, it was given the *Verbandkennzeichen* 1K+ -U.

Fighting along the Mius front intensified during mid-1943, with two Soviet offensives in the region in July and August. A third, which broke through German defences on 28 October, forced the new 6. Armee to withdraw behind the Dnieper; a retreat that effectively stranded the 17. Armee in the Crimea when the Soviets cut the German lines at the Isthmus of Perekop.

With the intensification of the battles on the Mius front, the *Staffel* was temporarily employed as a fighter bomber squadron alongside the III *Gruppe* of *Schlachtgeschwader* 3. At about the same time, the unit began receiving Heinkel He 111 aircraft, which during December 1943 and January 1944 were reinforced by elements of the I *Gruppe* of *Kampfgeschwader* 4. The primary objective was the interdiction of increasing Soviet naval activity in the Black Sea. On 11 January 1944, the unit celebrated its 2,000th operational sortie.

By mid-May 1944, Allied intelligence reported that the unit had on strength five Bf 110 (of which none were serviceable) and a further ten He 111 (of which just four were serviceable). To complement this, the *Staffel* had a total of six Messerschmitt and nine Heinkel-qualified crews. Allied intelligence was aware that on 13 May the unit had transferred three Bf 110s and their crew as replacements to II *Gruppe* of *Zestörergeschwader* 1. In fact so good was Allied intelligence, it was able to report with some confidence that the aircraft on strength were given the operational codes of 1K+BU, CU, DU, FU, HU, LU, MU, NU, OU, PU, QU, RU, SU, TU, UU, of which aircraft O, P, R, and S were positively identified as He 111s.

During the summer of 1944, the unit was increasingly relied upon for convoy escort duties in the north-west Black Sea. The He 111 detachment was further tasked with night reconnaissance in the area Constantsa-Sevastopol and then along the south coast of the Crimea as far as Tuapse. On the returning flight, crews were instructed to make bombing attacks in the Kuban area, especially the ports of Anapa and Novorossisk, which were supplying the Russian advance into the region. To aid in their operations, by 1944 the aircraft were fitted FuG 200 radar, while Allied intelligence had received word of Lichtenstein apparatus also being employed by the unit.

Still under the command of Klimmer, since he was promoted to *Hauptmann*, the *Staffel* fought increasingly lengthening odds as the Germans withdrew from Russia. By July 1944, the unit had transferred to Gossen, where it was redesignated as the 12 Staffel of Zestörergeschwader 26 on 18 July 1944. With no further need for a coastal reconnaissance unit in the east, the unit was not reformed.

Sonderstaffel Schwilden

Formed on 14 March 1940, *Sonderstaffel* Schwilden was equipped with He 59s. Under the command of *Hptm* Horst Schwilden, the unit was raised specifically for help in securing the bridges in Rotterdam on the morning of 10 May 1940. The aim was to deliver troops of the 11./*Infanterie-Regiment* 16 and sappers of the 2nd company of the Pioneer-Battalion to key points near the bridges to avert their destruction before the main invasion forces arrived.

On the morning of the invasion, the unit approached the Maas River in a pre-arranged pattern; they simultaneously landed six aircraft from the east and another six from the west. Landing under fire, the soldiers carried aboard the seaplanes were disgorged and rowed ashore in rubber assault dinghies. Despite the defence, the Germans had little difficulty securing their objectives; the operation took place at 04:00 hours, with the targets virtually unguarded.

After landing the troops, the He 59s had been moored along the Maas to act as air ambulances for any seriously wounded German soldiers that needed ferrying from the battle area. This presented a worthwhile target for the Danes, who during the morning sent two gunboats up the Maas to attack the Germans. Although beaten off, four aircraft involved were destroyed (WNr 1830, 1995, 2593, and 2599), while the remaining eight all received damage to varying degrees. With the conclusion of the operation, *Sonderstaffel* Schwilden was disbanded on 12 May 1940, and the remaining aircraft returned to *Höhere Fliegerausbildungskommando* 2 for distribution to training establishments.

15

Küstenfliegergruppe Stavanger

On 9 April 1940, the Germans launched *Unternehmen* Weserübung, the invasion of Denmark and Norway. While operations in Denmark lasted a mere 24 hours, the invasion of Norway was a more complex and drawn out affair. Although German forces quickly secured tenuous bridgeheads at various strategic points along the coastline of Norway on the opening day of the offensive, it became evident that British counter-attacks supported by the Royal Navy were likely to disrupt, if not entirely dislodge, the various footholds. As a result, it became increasingly clear that direct air support and reconnaissance units had to be brought forward to support operations on the ground. The disastrous naval losses at Narvik in the opening days of the campaign had in no small part been suffered for want of adequate air coverage, while the Allied landings at Namsos and Andalsnes in April had reinforced the need to strengthen German positions in central Norway.

Five weeks into the campaign for Norway, at the end of May 1940, the 3./406, 3./606, and 2./906 were redeployed to Stavanger. Overseeing the movement and operations of these units, F.d.L West created a new *Stabsstaffel*. Heading the new unit was the *Major beim Stabe* of *Küstenfliegergruppe 406, Maj.* Schwarz, from whom the new unit took its name *Gruppe* Schwarz. While the unit was not a flying unit, it oversaw the operations against Allied shipping in the North and Norwegian Sea and along the British coastline.

To prepare for the deployment from Hörnum to Stavanger of two *Staffeln* of Do 18 flying boats, there required an immediate investigation of the area to ascertain whether a Do 18 *Staffel* could be flown out of the harbour at Stavanger while the other remained operational from its base at Sola-Sea. Arriving two days in advance of the planned move by the 3./406 and 2./906, *Gruppe* Schwarz soon dismissed concerns raised about

The movement of troops along the stretch of Norwegian coastline required all transport aircraft available to be turned over to such operations. Here two He 59s of KGzbV 108 are at anchor in Stavanger harbour.

the size of the two bases' dispersal areas and adjacent mountains; at both seaplane bases, it was found that there was sufficient waterway length for a loaded Do 18 to perform a safe takeoff run even without the aide of wind assistance.[6]

At this time, an ordinary load for a Do 18 was considered to be 1,800 litres of fuel, two SC 50 bombs, and a single cannon. The weight of these was considered insufficient to present a problem for operations from either base. The adjacent mountains, especially at Stavanger, were not considered of sufficient height to create any undue cause for concern for daylight takeoffs and landings. However, owing to numerous islands and rocky outcrops located around the dispersal area and the insufficient number of emergency lights available for night takeoffs and landings, operations conducted after dark were not considered possible. However at the time, the restrictions placed upon night flying were not seen to cause any great concern given the intended duration of operations compared with the shortness of the Norwegian nights.[7] As a result, *Maj*. Schwarz did not consider that combat readiness of any of the two *Staffeln* based in Norwegian waters would be unduly affected.

At both Stavanger and Sola-Sea, the ground infrastructure met the German requirements as far as accommodation and catering were concerned. However, when the advanced party arrived at both locations they found there was insufficient number of dispersal points. Construction on these began almost immediately and was completed in a very short space of time. Yet the biggest problem faced at both bases was the lack of service boats. As the unit's war diary dryly noted on 29 May 1940, If operations are to be maintained then the transfer of two service boats of the C3-class to both Stavanger and Sola-See is necessary.'

A further difficulty faced by the Germans was the lack of space and technical equipment (i.e. plane lifts) for the exchanging of engines or small repair work. However, it was found that an elevator (hoist) device under construction at Sola-See would soon become operational, while at Stavanger a mobile derrick crane could be used for as an interim solution. Furthermore, the Germans soon discovered that at Sola-Stavanger the slipway was serviceable, and by employing a strong tractor a Do 18 could be dragged ashore for maintenance work. As a final stop-gap, *Maj.* Schwarz and his team deemed the small repair works at Sola suitable for basic repairs if manned by a detachment of Bachmann-Aircraft Works Ribnitz Company employees.

Overshadowing all these considerations, the new unit's primary concern was the arranging of spare part stocks. While the Germans had access to some replacement parts aboard the steamer the *Hannover*, *Maj.* Schwarz had no way of telling 'how many spare parts are available on board the steamship'.

The surrounding countryside at Stavanger was not considered dangerous to operations, while the almost constant daylight in the summer months allowed for constant activity.

While it was not a serious concern, the deployment of the two flying boat *Staffeln* created problems for the crews. Living quarters of both the flying and ground personnel of each *Staffeln* were separated. Owing to a lack of experience, the effect of this problem, although not easily assessed, was a concern. With replacement crews and minimal experience of the Norwegian coastline, crews found it difficult to learn from each other given the segregation of their respective facilities. As *Maj.* Schwarz later commented, it was desirable that, 'Personnel should be accommodated together due to various combat and discipline reasons.'

So as to turn the various *Staffeln* under the command of the new unit over to combat operations as quickly as possible, *Gruppe* Schwarz was supported by the ship the *Karl Meier*, which was equipped with a wireless station that could fulfill all requirements for a combat ground wireless station. However, the radio sets aboard the vessel, although operational on all combat frequencies, was useful only between sundown till sunrise. During the day, it was found that radio communications with Germany or deployed aircraft could not be guaranteed given the high volume of traffic.

With preliminary arrangements completed, on 31 May 1940 the transfer of the units commenced. During the day, eight Do 18s each from 3./406 and 2./906 deployed to the region. These flying boats were supplemented by three Do 17Z land-based bombers that transferred from Copenhagen to Sola-land during the day.

With the campaign in Norway winding down, much of the *Gruppe*'s activities were focused on maritime reconnaissance and anti-submarine patrols in support of German shipping operating along the coast of Norway. To this end, each day, weather permitting, the two flying boat units each furnished an average of four sorties. Primarily, the operational load out of the aircraft was 1,900 litres of fuel and two SC 250 bombs. However, on occasion the fuel limit was increased when longer-ranging reconnaissance operations were required. On these rare occasions, the aircraft carried either two SC 50s or none at all, depending upon whether or not enemy submarine activity was anticipated. Typically, each operation was conducted along three legs, forming a triangular shape over a given area. Each aircraft operated individually, which on occasions gave rise to difficult situations.

Early on 4 June 1940, *Gruppe* Stavanger ordered a reconnaissance patrol by four crews each from 3./406 and 2./906 to the north of Stavanger. Taking off in the early afternoon, the crews quickly encountered fog between 0°30′ E to 3°30′ E, and 59°30′ N to 61°40′ N. At 16:20 hours local time, 8L+LK (WNr 790) of the 2./906 reported it had been attacked by an unidentified type. Eight minutes later, *Uffz* Karl Stockinger, the radio operator, sent out a distress signal. However, the inexperience of the radio operators stationed aboard the *Gruppe's* command ship the *Karl Meier*, combined with interference from surrounding terrain, meant Stockinger's calls for assistance remained unanswered. Fortuitously for Stockinger and his crew, the radio operator aboard 8L+CK, on patrol in the vicinity, picked up the distress call and turned towards the scene. In what proved a catalogue of disaster, the observer of 8L+CK wrongly transcribed the location and arrived to search a grid approximately 30 nautical miles north of 8L+LK's true position. Meanwhile, aboard 8L+LK the crew was faced with the grim reality of ditching in the North Sea. The surprise attack, which had been delivered by Flt Lt Mitchell in Blenheim R3629 of 254 Squadron, had severely damaged the Dornier. Alighting on the sea, the crew scrambled into the dingy to await rescue. For Stockinger and the remainder of his crew, the wait would be a long one. With the *Gruppe* aboard the *Karl Meier* oblivious to the situation and 8L+CK searching some distance away, the possibility for survival looked grim. In the end, Stockinger, *Fw* Klare (Bm), and *ObFw* Lippert (F) were all rescued by U-47. Unfortunately, the observer *Lt* Hans Weinling was killed during the ditching procedure and was buried at sea.

The dangers of operating alone over such a hostile environment were further emphasised two days later. Again, *Gruppe* Schwarz ordered reconnaissance activities by four aircraft each from 3./406 and 2./906, each armed with two SC 250 bombs and fuelled with 1,800 litres. The

Of prime importance to *Küstenfliegergruppen* operations was the protection of shipping and convoys routed through Norwegian waters.

takeoff that was timed for 02:00 hours had been postponed due to a fog that settled around midnight in the area of Stavanger and Sola. The meteorological branch forecast the fog would clear around 06:00 hours and so Gruppe Schwarz ordered the eight crews to establish takeoff readiness from 06:00 hours onwards. However, by 06:00 hours the sea swell was such that it would prove difficult to launch the aircraft, and so a further postponement, this time of 4 hours, was ordered. Finally, at 13:00 hours the situation had cleared sufficiently that the ordered reconnaissance could be given the go ahead.

Not long after the aircraft were launched, 8L+IK and 8L+DK both suffered technical difficulties with their Jumo engines, forcing their early return. Following standard procedure, the crew of IK did not report their condition and instead maintained radio silence. This meant IK's assigned reconnaissance grid remained un-patrolled. Perhaps recognising such an event, the crew of DK decided to notify *Gruppe* Schwarz of their early return, and the duties for reconnoitering their grid were handed over to a third aircraft in the operation, 8L+CK. However, in a repeat of the incident on 4 June, the difficulties in managing the radio operations aboard the *Karl Meier* meant that the crew aboard 8L+CK was only informed about their additional requirements some 2 hours after DK had turned for Stavanger. The difficulty in maintaining adequate contact between *Gruppe* Schwarz and aircraft on patrol remained a constant problem.

The difficulties endured during early June were not restricted to radio and navigational errors. On 8 June 1940, a reconnaissance operation flown by 7T+EL of the 3./606 sighted an enemy convoy west of Stavanger at 11:30 hours. As the aircraft circled, *Gruppe* Schwarz received an update from the crew 15 minutes later, reporting that the convoy consisted of eight ships supported by four destroyers. Having furnished sufficient details to vector other aircraft towards the convoy, EL rolled in for the attack, armed with SC 50 bombs. However, a technical problem with the bomb release system precluded the observer from jettisoning his bombs on the first run. Despite this, the pilot of EL circled the convoy and made ready for another attack. However, as the aircraft dropped out of cloud cover it received damage to the wings by what was thought to be 3.7-cm flak. This, combined with the dubious reliability of the bomb release mechanism, was sufficient reason for the crew of EL to abandon the attack. As EL was turning away from the convoy, a sister aircraft, 7T+FL, was attacking three patrol boats in a nearby sector. Although the crew recorded no signs of success in their attack, the aircraft was also damaged by flak from the vessels.

Perhaps more worrying for *Gruppe* Schwarz was the growing list of losses suffered by the unit for minimal results. On 10 June 1940, Do 17Z 7T+BL of the 3./606 engaged a Sunderland over the North Sea. During the

Unlike in Denmark, the Germans found it difficult going in Norway. Stretched supply lines, British counter-landings and constant calls for air activity placed a great strain on various units. Here He 111H-3 of 8./KG 26 (1H+ES) lies at rest at the edge of the runway at Oslo/Fornebau on 12 April 1940, after a landing accident. It was damaged beyond what was considered economically repairable.

combat, the observer *Lt.z.S* Pricker was killed, and the flight engineer *Uffz* Hölscher was wounded. It was only through the skill of *Ofw* Gerbig, the pilot, that the aircraft managed to return to base. Meanwhile, on 11 June Do 18G 8L+HK (WNr 819) crashed on landing, killing all but the flight mechanic *Uffz* Walter Ernst.

Two days later at 21:00 hours, command of the *Gruppe* was officially handed over to *Maj.* Stockmann. *Maj.* Schwarz returned to Hörnum, where he took over command of the remaining elements of *Küstenfliegergruppe* 406. Accompanying the change in command, *F.d.L West* ordered the change in designation for the unit. On 14 June 1940, *Gruppe* Schwarz was renamed *Küstenfliegeruppe* Stavanger. Organisationally nothing changed and the new unit continued to operate in the same fashion as its predecessor. However, with the campaign in Norway having been successfully concluded, the operational focus of combat sorties conducted by the various *Staffeln* under the *Gruppe*'s command was increasingly widened in search of enemy shipping, submarine, and aerial reconnaissance activity.

Throughout June, *Küstenfliegergruppe* Stavanger continued to oversee operations and function in a normal manner. While occasional sightings of British submarines, such as on 28 June when *Hptm* Schriek of 2./106 – a newly subordinated unit to the *Gruppe* – reportedly damaged an enemy submarine in the Skagerrak, the majority of offensive action was against enemy merchant shipping. As June gave way to July, the *Gruppe* increasingly found itself playing a role in convoy escort duties. In this role, the unit's various *Staffeln* came into increasing contact with other units, such as *Küstenfliegergruppe* 506 and *Bordfliegergruppe* 196, which were similarly tasked with defensive operations. Given the increasing role in defending German shipping along the coast of Norway and across the Skagerrak, it was only fitting that the last major engagement the *Gruppe* participated in was the sortie by the heavy surface ships *Gneisenau* and *Nürnberg*, escorted by the destroyers *Hans Lody*, *Friedrich Ihn*, *Paul Jacobi*, and *Karl Galster,* and torpedo boats *Luchs*, *Iltis*, *Kondor*, *Jaguar*, and *T5* from Drontheim. The operation commenced on 25 July 1940. Two days later, *Küstenfliegergruppe* Stavanger was disbanded and its members reformed as Küstenfliegergruppe (Stab) 706.

Endnotes

1. Built in 1895 the vessel weighed 5984GRT. The vessel was adapted for aircraft operations by the addition of a long flat deck installed on the bow of the ship in 1911.

2. There are discrepancies in these figures, thus the more popular figures have been cited here.

3. By November only 2./606 was operational so the loss was more theoretical than realistic.

4. Both *KüFlGr* 306 and 406 used K6 as its *Verbandkennzeich*. This was due to the fact that *KüFlGr* 306 had no *Stabstaffel* and was instead attached to *KüFlGr* 406.

5. Narodnyy Komissariat Vnutrennikh Del. The Russian Secret Police and forerunner of the KGB.

6. The 3./606 was equipped with Do 17Z landplanes and was based at Kiel-Holtenau at this time, however elements of the Staffel were deployed to Sola-land on 31 May 1940.

7. During clear sky periods in June, darkness is between 23.30 and 02.00 hours Norwegian Time.

Select Bibliography

Books and Articles

Balke, U. *Die Küstenstaffel Krim* (Jet Prop, 1995)

Barker, R. *Hurricats* (Stroud: Tempus Publishing, 2005)

Bekker, C. *The Luftwaffe War Diaries* (New York: Da Capo Press, 1994)

Claasen, A. *Hitler's Northern War* (Kansas: Kansas University Press, 2001)

Corum, J. *The Luftwaffe: Creating the Operational Air War* (Kansas: Kansas University Press, 1997)

The Spanish Civil War: Lessons Learned and Not Learned by the Great Powers (Journal of Military History, 1998)

Foreman, J. *The Forgotten Months* (New Malden: Air Research Publications, 1998)

Part 1 and 2 (Walton on Thames: Air Research Publications, 1941)

Goss, C. *Luftwaffe Fighters and Bombers* (Mechanicsburg: Stackpole Books, 2000)

Homze, E. *Arming the Luftwaffe* (Nebraska: University of Nebraska Press, 1976)

Hooton, E. *Phoenix Triumphant* (London: Brockhampton Press, 1994)

Eagle in Flames (London: Brockhampton Press, 1999)

Hümmelchen, G. *Die deutschen Seeflieger: 1935-1945* (München: J. F. Lehmanns Verlag, 1976)

Isby, D. (ed.) *The Luftwaffe and the War at Sea* (London: Chatham Publishing, 2005)

Kington, J. and F. S. *Wekusta* (Ottringham: Flight Recorder Publications, 2006)

Layman, R. *Naval Aviation in the First World War* (London: Chatham Publishing, 2002)

López, R. and C. O'Donnell. *Seaplanes of the Legion Condor* (Atglen: Schiffer, 2009)

Merrick, K. *Luftwaffe Camouflage and Markings*. Vol. 2. (London: Chevron Publishing, 2005)

Meyer, H. *Erlebnisse eines Seefliegers* (Germany: Aviatik, 1991)

Neitzel, S. *Der Einsatz der deutschen Luftwaffe über dem Atlantik und der Nordsee* (Bonn: Bernard and Graefe Verlag, 1995)

Ramsey, W. *The Blitz Then and Now*, Vol. 1, 2, and 3 (London: Battle of Britain Prints International)

Rohwer, J. *Chronology of the War at Sea* (London: Chatham Publishing, 2005)

Shores, C. *Fledgling Eagles* (London: Grubb Street, 1998)

Thiele, H. *Luftwaffe Aerial Torpedo Aircraft and Operations* (Crowborough: Hikoki, 2004)

Ulman, M. *Luftwaffe Colours* (Ottringham: Hikoki, 2002)

Urbanke, A. *Die deutschen Magnetminen-Abwurfeinsätze im Westen von Oktober 1939-Oktober 1940* (Bad Zwischenahn: Luftwaffe Im Focus, 2007)

Official Documents

National Archives and Records Administration

Kriegstagebuch Küstenfliegergruppe der Küstenfliegergruppe 106. PG
  80025-034, roll 3327 (Aug 1939-Apr 1940)

Kriegstagebuch des Küstenfliegerstaffels. I/106. PG 80035-046, rolls 3327-
  28 (Aug 1939-Sep 1940)

  II/106. PG 80047-058, roll 3328 (Aug 1939-Apr 1940)

  III/106. PG 80059-065, roll 3328 (Sep 1939-Apr 1940)

Kriegstagebuch der Küstenfliegergruppe 306 (later 406). PG 80066-068,
  roll 3328 (Aug-Oct 1939)

Kriegstagebuch des Küstenfliegerstaffels II/306 (later III/406). PG 80069-
  071, rolls 3328-29 (Aug-Oct 1939:)

Kriegstagebuch der Küstenfliegergruppe 406. PG 80072-082, rolls 3354-
  55 (Aug 1939-Dec 1940)

Kriegstagebuch des Küstenfliegerstaffels. I/406. PG 80083-086, roll 3355
  (Aug 1939-Jan 1940)

  II/406. PG 80087-091, rolls 3355-56 (Aug 1939-Apr 1940)

  III/406. PG 80092-097, roll 3356 (Aug 1939-Apr 1940)

Kriegstagebuch der Küstenfliegergruppe 606. PG 80146-157, roll 3356
  (Mar-Sep 1940)

Kriegstagebuch des Küstenfliegerstaffels I/606. PG 80158-161, roll 3356
  (Aug 1939-Mar 1940)

Kriegstagebuch der Küstenfliegergruppe 706, Oct 1939. PG 80162-165,
  rolls 3356-57 (Jul 1940-Mar 1941)

Kriegstagebuch des Küstenfliegerstaffels I/706. PG 80167-183, rolls 3357-
  58 (Sep-Oct 1939, May-Jul 1940, Nov 1941-Mar 1942)

Kriegstagebuch der Küstenfliegergruppe 806 (later 506). PG 80072-132, rolls 3329-31 (Aug 1939-Apr 1940, Sep 1940-Mar 1942)

Kriegstagebuch des Küstenfliegerstaffels. I/506. PG 80133-135, roll 3331 (Oct 1939-Mar 1940)

II/506. PG 80136-137, roll 3332 (Aug 1939-Mar 1940)

III/506. PG 80138-145, roll 3332 (Sep 1939-Apr 1940)

II/806. PG 80189-191, roll 3358 (Nov-Dec 1939, Feb-Apr 1940)

III/806. PG 80192, roll 3358 (Jan-Apr 1940)

Kriegstagebuch der Küstenfliegergruppe 906 (later 706). PG 80193-214, rolls 3332-34 (Aug 1939-Oct 1941)

Kriegstagebuch des Küstenfliegerstaffels. I/906. PG 80215-216, roll 3334 (Aug 1939-Mar 1940)

II/906. PG 80217-218, rolls 3334-35 (Oct 1939-Apr 1940)

III/906. PG 80219-220, roll 3335 (Nov 1939-Mar 1940)

Kriegstagebuch der Gruppe Schwarz (special air reconnaissance group established under FdL West at Stavanger). no PG (file KR 3095), filmed with PG 95622, roll 4270

Kriegstagebuch der Küstenfliegergruppe Stavanger. PG 80021-024, roll 3354 (Jun-Jul 1940)

Kriegstagebuch des Sonderstaffels Tr.O. (special squadron of Do 26 aircraft assigned to air/sea rescue duties, operating at different times from Brest, Trondheim, and Tränemünde).   PG 80309-313, roll 3335 (Feb-Mar and Jul-Sep 1939)

Australian War Memorial

'The Role of the German Air Force in the War at Sea'. AWM 54 423/4/103. Part 7

'Proposal for the Conduct of Aerial Warfare Against Great Britain, 22 November 1939'. AWM 54 423/4/103. Part 20

'German Air Attacks on PQ Convoys, Extracts from Luftlfotte 5 Kriegstagebuch, 9/42'. AWM 54 423/4/103. Part 45

'Luftwaffe Strength and Serviceability Tables'. AWM 54 423/4/103. Part 100

'Operational Use of the Luftwaffe in the War At Sea'. AWM 423/4/103. Part 106

Public Records Office

'Daily Reports on GAF Bomber and Reconnaissance Activity'. HW 13/96 - 98

'Y Service Monthly Reports'. NA AIR 40/2355

Websites

Evans, P. *The Luftwaffe Experten Message Board* (2013)
   http://www.luftwaffe-experten.com

Holm, M. *The Luftwaffe 1933-1945* (1997-2000)
   http://ww2.dk/

Horta, R. *12 O'Clock High* (2000-2013)
   http://forum.12oclockhigh.net/